**NEW WINDOWS**

*I love books that are easy to read and understand, that lift our spirits, teach something of great value, contain meaningful stories, quote wise people, recommend other good books, and make us think about what's really important. Eureka! This one has it all. Thank you, Mark Matteson, for sharing your story. It will enrich the lives of all who read it.*

—Hal Urban, author, *The Power of Good News: Feeding Your Mind with What's Good for Your Heart* and *Life's Greatest Lessons: 20 Things That Matter*

*Mark Matteson continues to expand his reader's probability of greater success and happiness by asking 52 very probing questions.* An Old Light Through New Windows *is a great template for exploring yourself spiritually and opening new windows to what matters in life. Mark is a storytelling machine, weaving in humor and real-life examples to support each chapter's life lesson. I thoroughly enjoyed reading it, but appreciated more the reflection that happened after reading it. It changed my perspective and influenced me to become a better person and leader. Well done . . . and thank you!*

—Paul Kelly, Regional CEO of Wrench Group

*The most significant and enduring lesson my father taught me was, "You can tell how smart a person is, not by the answers they have, but by the questions they ask." This philosophy has consistently served me throughout my life. I am using Mark's new book for my personal and professional growth. Every Monday morning I will randomly select a question from his book and make that the focus of my week. I'd invite you to do the same. And have fun with it!*

—Nancy D. Solomon, author of *Impact! What Every Woman Needs to Know to Go from Invisible to Invincible.*

*Mark's new book will pull you in and keep you reading. I could not put it down. It's loaded with great stories, life-changing questions, and insights. Buy copies for everyone you care about. They will thank you.*

—Adam Christing, speaker, magician, and author of *Your Life is a Joke*

*I don't know anyone more committed to learning about personal development, putting his learning into practice, and helping other people grow than Mark Matteson. He has spent thousands of hours studying high-performing people and has humbly worked to improve himself using what he has learned. His personal-development experience gives him a passion for helping others grow and makes him a* tremendous resource for anyone committed to living an exceptional life. Read this book with a pen in hand—you will want to take notes.

—Andrew Bennett, two-time TED Talk presenter, magician, consultant

Join Mark for this engaging and insightful journey to realizing your greatest potential by doing some deep personal work guided in a fun, loving, and safe way that is unique to him. Read this book. It will change the way you see the world.

—Kenny Chapman, founder of The Blue Collar Success Group and podcast host of Leadership in a Nutshell.

In An Old Light Through New Windows, Mark Matteson poses wise questions that remind us to live authentically and pay attention to the choices we make. This is one of those books that you want to keep handy—for inspiration, motivation, and aspiration. Mark's positivity is infectious—catch it!

—Donna Cameron, author of A Year of Living Kindly

*If you have fifteen minutes a week, Mark Matteson has fifty-two questions to help you blow past mediocrity and build an exceptional life!*
—Anthony Michalski, publisher, KallistiPublishing.com

*Mark Matteson has us invest in 52 pieces of gold. Through his personal stories and sage wisdom from his mentors, he challenges us to look inward and make sure we are setting the bar high for ourselves. Mark uses questions and provocative statements to guide each of us to determine our own calling and future.*
—Tom Jackson, president, Jackson Systems

*Mark's done it again! Even after writing numerous wonderful books, he's written another gem. While most folks are seeking answers, Mark demonstrates that our answers are only as good as our questions. And it serves us well to learn to ask better questions if we'd like a better life. At 52 questions, we can focus on one insightful question per week and be living a remarkable life in a year. Or less. Mark is a true blessing. And that's not a question. It's a fact.*
—Kevin Knebl, international speaker, author, trainer, coach

*The old light is brighter than ever . . . I'd suggest you read (and better yet, write in) this book. I think you'll find your light gets brighter too.*

—Andy Armstrong, president, Base Solutions

*As we emerge from the COVID-19 pandemic, perspective is everything. We can't always control what happens to us, but we can control how we react so that we not only survive but thrive in our new normal. Mark's 52 questions helped me to step back and reassess, to look through that new window. Life is good and full of opportunity. Thanks, Mark!*

—Tim Brink, CEO, MCA

*I've known Mark Matteson almost thirty years. I'm fortunate to count him as a good friend. Don't be in a hurry to devour this smart, smart book.*

*Let it grow on you slowly. It's dense with life lessons. You cannot absorb them all at once. Keep reading . . . the questions become their own reward.*

*Then make a judgment. You'll return to this book often.*

—Bill Angle, president, Willard Marine

*I have read all of Mark's books and this one hits it out of the park. Do yourself a favor: Read it, apply the lessons in the book, and give it to all your family, friends, coworkers, and watch people's lives change because of it.*

*Once I started I couldn't stop. Not only did I finish this book in record time but I have committed to reading it daily. Wow!!! An absolutely amazing book.*

—Kelly Schols, author, speaker, coach, success mentor

*I've known Mark from the speaking circuit for nearly two decades. He always delivers compelling content with originality and verve! This book will change your life. Enjoy.*

—Michael Angelo Caruso, author of *Work Hacks— 30+ Ways to Speed Career Success*

# OLD LIGHT

## Through

# NEW WINDOWS

## ALSO BY MARK MATTESON

*Freedom from Fear*
*Freedom from Fear Forever*
*A Simple Choice*
*It's About TIME*
*Freedom from FAT*

### EBOOKS

*Wag More, Bark Less*
*Sales Success Stories*
*Customer Service Excellence*
*Presenting Like a Pro*
*You Don't Have to be Sick To Get Better*
*Sparking Sales Success (How to Enjoy a 75% Close Ratio)*

# MARK MATTESON

# OLD LIGHT
## *Through*
# NEW WINDOWS

**Ugly Dog Publishing**

Published by **Ugly Dog Publishing,** Edmonds, WA

ISBN 978-0-9995350-4-2

Printed in the United States of America

*For my grandchildren, Penelope, Sawyer and Ronin. I love you more today than yesterday, but not as much as tomorrow.*

*And to my parents, Robert D. Matteson and Barbara Jean Matteson, for giving me the gift of life and, by your able example, showing me the way. Thank you from the bottom of my heart. I miss you every day.*

# CONTENTS

# FOREWORD

# by Hal Urban

*Mark, you sure messed up my plans for the day—in a really good way! I was going to skim your manuscript, come up with some pithy little plug for your new book, and send it to you before getting to my daily chores.*

*The "skim" turned into a full read, and I enjoyed every page. Fabulous! Thank you for saving me from my chores.*

*I couldn't help thinking this: 52 chapters—if some person (especially a young man or woman, one who wants to live a good life) read and studied one chapter a week, answered all the questions at the end, then re-read the chapter, he or she would be a thousand times wiser.*

*After much consideration, here is the first draft of my endorsement:*

*"I love books that are easy to read and understand, that lift our spirits, teach something of great value, contain meaningful stories, quote wise people, recommend other good books, and make us think about what's really important. Eureka! This one has it all. Thank you,*

*Mark Matteson for sharing your story. It will enrich the lives of all who read it."*

*Having said that—We have a lot in common my friend: our positive philosophies of life, speaking, writing, books we've read, three sons, even basketball. I went to the University of San Francisco (Jesuit like your Seattle U) on a basketball scholarship. Alas, I wasn't good enough to play in the NBA. My destiny seemed to be teaching young people—no regrets.*

*Also hope you sell millions of copies of this amazing book. It's going to change lives . . .*

—**Hal Urban,** author, *The Power of Good News: Feeding Your Mind with What's Good for Your Heart* and *Life's Greatest Lessons: 20 Things That Matter*

# INTRODUCTION

**My father used to say,** "Getting older isn't for sissies." At the time—in my early forties—I was launching a new speaking business, raising three boys, flipping houses, traveling like crazy, writing my third book, and running like my hair was on fire. When someone would ask me how I was, I'd reply "At 200 miles per hour, I don't have any friends . . ." Now that wasn't true, I am happy to report I did, and still do, have lots of friends. But I couldn't relate to my father's point of view. Now that my boys are having children of their own, I am *shining an old light through new windows.* I understand with age comes challenges—but I prefer to focus on what is great about my life at sixty-three years young. I have made more than my fair share of mistakes. I've had one setback after another. I have lived long enough to gain some perspective, a new set of glasses if you will. I'm a grandfather now—same old light, brand new windows. I have learned that the quality of my life reflects the kind of questions I have asked myself.

James Thurber once said, *"It's better to know some of the questions than all of the answers."*

Socrates believed that philosophy should achieve practical results for the greater well-being of society. He attempted to establish an ethical system based on human reason rather than theological doctrine. Socrates pointed out that human choice was motivated by the desire for happiness. He is credited with the *Socratic method*, the art of asking open-ended questions that uncover ideas, perspectives, solutions and, hopefully, a change in behavior. Asking the right questions leads to new answers.

Tony Robbins once said, *"Successful people ask better questions—as a result they get better answers."* What questions lead to our biggest breakthroughs and successes?

In this book, we will see how certain questions shape our thinking and how personal and organizational problems can often be traced to the kinds of questions we ask ourselves and our organization.

I have been interviewing successful people since the eighth grade when I was cut from my junior high basketball team. Through every chapter of my life I sought out men and women who had done what I wanted to do and been where I wanted to go. *Mentors.* I approached them and asked, "Just how did you get so good at what you do?"

Now that I am a podcaster and publisher, I ask my guests and writing clients some simple questions—after doing some research first.

1) Why do you think you have had so much success?
2) What do you do that your competition does not do?
3) What books should I be reading?
4) What seminars should I attend?
5) Who had the biggest impact on you coming up?
6) What advice would you offer someone just starting out?
7) How do you handle setbacks and adversity?
8) What would you want people to know about you?
9) How do you want to be remembered?
10) What is the most important business lesson you have ever learned?

In this book, I have chosen questions that might just stimulate your thinking. Maybe, *just maybe*, I can get you excited and inspire you to change, grow, and become a better version of yourself. My sincere hope is that some of these questions will put a rock in your shoe to remind you to think of a few new things, and question what you're doing and where you're going.

George Bernard Shaw lived to be ninety-five. He wrote four hours every day. He had a unique perspective on life. He once wrote, *"Life isn't about finding yourself. Life is about creating yourself. We don't stop playing because we grow old; we grow old because we stop playing. Progress is impossible without change, and those who cannot change their minds cannot change anything. Youth is wasted on the young. A life spent making mistakes is not only more honorable, but more useful than a life spent doing nothing. The single biggest problem in communication is the illusion that it has taken place. Some men see things as they are and ask why. Others dream things that never were and ask why not. Beware of false knowledge; it is more dangerous than ignorance."*

Oh, and the fifty-two questions? You'll find one at the end of every chapter.

Now let's get started . . .

# WHO AM I?

*Window One*

*The two most important days in your life are the day you were born and the day you find out why.* —Mark Twain

**Who am I?** How did I become the person I am? What influenced my values, beliefs, habits, and attitudes? Who were my biggest positive influences from my childhood? If our life is a novel, examining each chapter is vital to understanding the person we've become.

Re-reading Bruce Springsteen's memoir, *Born to Run,* which took him seven years to write, gives us a partial glimpse into the answer. Writing with a kind of brutal honesty few authors do, he posits:

*Those whose love we wanted but could not get, we emulate. It is dangerous but makes us feel closer, gives us an illusion of the intimacy we never had. It stakes our claim upon that which was rightfully ours but denied. In my twenties as my song and my story began to take shape, I searched for the voice I would blend with mine to do the telling. It is a moment when through creativity and will, you rework, repossess and rebirth the conflicting voices of your childhood, to turn them into something alive, powerful and seeking light. I'm a repairman. That's part of my job. So I, who'd never done a week's worth of manual labor in my life (hail, hail rock and roll!), put on a factory worker's clothes, my father's clothes, and went to work.*

When I consider the professional path I chose over twenty-five years ago as a speaker and writer, and I reflect back upon my parents' natural and lifelong affinities, my own path becomes crystal clear. I am my father's son. He was a tremendous athlete, all-state in three sports. He went on to coach every sport when, as athletic director of an Air Force base in Yokohama, Japan, he inspired, encouraged, and taught men the value of hard work, commitment to the team, and the value of selfless dedication to winning.

My career as a corporate coach, consultant, teacher, and speaker had its roots in my father's love of sports. I watched sports with my father on TV hundreds of times. When I committed to basketball at thirteen, it was my dad who built the backyard court. We played HORSE and one-on-one until our respective competitive juices clashed like the titans of old. With my father, everything was a competition, even cribbage!

My mother had a passion for the arts. She loved music, plays, community theater, films, especially musicals. Psychologists claim the person you are by age five is who you will be the rest of your life. What I consistently heard coming through the stereo speakers at that impressionable age was showtunes: *West Side Story, The King and I, Oklahoma.* When we lived in Japan, my mother was an extra in a few films, including one of Woody Allen's early pictures, *What's up, Tiger Lily?*, a low-rent Japanese spy flick with dubbed dialogue. Later in life she did community theater. She was also a voracious reader of books and magazines and kept a journal her whole life. Her secret ambition was to write a book. Her memoir—all twenty copies of it—was self-published just before she died.

When I consider these influences, the writing, coaching, and acting, it's easy to see how I gravitated to speaking, coaching, consulting and, yes, becoming an author, publisher, and podcaster.

When I step on a stage to teach, coach, inspire, and entertain, I am channeling my parents. Bruce Springsteen was right. I put on my father's clothes and go to work.

Who are you? Why are you here? How did your parents influence you?

I know who I am. How about you?

## Your Ah-has? List Your Lights

*"Who am I? I am . . ."*

_____

_____

_____

_____

_____

_____

_____

_____

_____

_____

_____

_____

_____

_____

_____

_____

_____

## *Window Two*

# WHAT DID YOU LOVE TO DO WHEN YOU WERE SEVEN?

*Follow your bliss and the universe will open doors where there were only walls.* —Joseph Campbell

**By the time I was seven years old** I had a passion for blocks and forts, miniature plastic army men, and building battle scenes. I would be lost for hours in my own little world of make-believe. I was building something special. I would plead for my parents to keep it "Set Up." Most of the time, no matter how special my battle scene was, at the end of the day it all went back in the box.

As I reflect back upon the various businesses I have had, what mattered was the building of them. The juice was the work, the ideas, the creativity, the "set up" of it all. Various hobbies captured my imagination over the years: a large collection of army men, baseball cards, LP records, DVDs, hats of all kinds. Now I collect clients. I guess you could call me a serious collector.

Director Michael Apted created a series of documentaries, called the *Up* series, over a fifty-year period in which he revisited the same group of British-born subjects in seven-year intervals. The subjects are interviewed about the changes that had occurred in their lives during the last seven years. In the fifth film, he draws a fascinating conclusion, granted from a relatively small sample size—however, he claims, *"The children who were doing the things they claimed they loved at seven, at age thirty-five were the most successful and most fulfilled."*

My sophomore year, when I was fourteen, I heard a former state championship basketball coach speak at our high school. He lit a fire under me. I attended a two-day seminar he conducted a few weeks later at Seattle University. Two years later he spoke to our team. When I was thirty-four I attended a two-day business seminar he conducted. Two years after that I went to work for him for almost four years. I watched him present hundreds of times. I stayed in touch with him right up until the day he died. When I speak, I am channeling my mentor, Bob Moawad.

He is alive and well in the keynotes and seminars I conduct around the world. In a very real sense, he gave me permission to follow my bliss. I owe him a great deal.

I remember watching a PBS special with Bill Moyers and Joseph Campbell . . .

BILL MOYERS: *Do you ever have the sense of . . . being helped by hidden hands?*

JOSEPH CAMPBELL: *All the time. It is miraculous. I even have a superstition that has grown on me as a result of invisible hands coming all the time, namely, that if you do follow your bliss you put yourself on a kind of track that has been there all the while, waiting for you, and the life that you ought to be living is the one you are living. When you can see that, you begin to meet people who are in your field of bliss, and they open doors to you. I say, follow your bliss and don't be afraid, and doors will open where you didn't know they were going to be.*

Joseph Campbell was a life-long student and teacher of the human spirit and mythology—not just the mythology of cultures long dead, but of living myth, as it made itself known in the work of modern artists and philosophers—individuals who searched within themselves and their societies to identify the need about which they were passionate. He called this burning need that they sought to quench *fulfilling their bliss*.

When Campbell died, just months after recording the interviews with Bill Moyers that were to become *The Power of Myth*, he had no idea how these interviews and, in particular, this idea of following one's bliss, would resonate with the public. Within months of airing on PBS in the United States, *Follow your bliss* had become a catchphrase.

Yet it is important to note that following one's bliss, as Campbell saw it, isn't merely a matter of doing whatever you like, and certainly not doing simply as you are told. It is a matter of identifying that pursuit which you are truly passionate about and attempting to give yourself absolutely to it (It's as much about *blisters* as *bliss*). In so doing, you will find your fullest potential and serve your community to the greatest possible extent.

If you follow your bliss you put yourself on a kind of track that has been there all the while, waiting for you, and the life that you ought to be living is the one you *are* living. Wherever you are, if you are following your bliss you are enjoying that refreshment, that life within you, all the time.

I followed my bliss as a passionate part-time avocation for years. Then one day, I committed to it 100% and have never looked back. I have the blisters to prove it!

My children never played with plastic army men. They had the Teenage Mutant Ninja Turtles—"Heroes in a Half Shell." We all need heroes. They open doors.

No matter what game you play in life and business, in the end it all goes back in the box. Make certain you are playing *your* game before it's too late.

## Your Ah-has? List Your Lights

*"What is my bliss?"*

_____

_____

_____

_____

_____

_____

_____

_____

_____

_____

_____

_____

_____

_____

_____

_____

*Window Three*

# WHAT ARE YOU GRATEFUL FOR?

*Gratitude unlocks the fullness of life. It turns what we have into enough, and more. It turns denial into acceptance, chaos to order, and confusion to clarity. It can turn a meal into a feast, a house into a home, a stranger into a friend. Gratitude makes sense of our past, brings peace for today, and creates a vision for tomorrow.*
—Melodie Beatty

**Gratitude is an action word.** Take your gratitude and put it on your feet.

The science of psychoneuroimmunology, introduced to a wider audience by Norman Cousins in the 1980s through his bestselling book *Anatomy of An Illness as Perceived by the Patient*, proves that gratitude affects our health.

From the Norman Cousins Center's website: *The Norman Cousins Center for Psychoneuroimmunology at UCLA investigates the interactions between the brain and the body, the role of psychological well-being for health and recovery from illness, and the translation of such knowledge into effective behavioral strategies that prevent disease, promote healing and enhance well-being across the life span.*

Positive emotions strengthen our immune system, which enables us to resist disease and recover more quickly from illness. Gratitude, optimism, and laughter all serve to release endorphins into the bloodstream. Endorphins are the body's natural painkillers that stimulate dilation of the blood vessels, which leads to a relaxed heart. Conversely, negative emotions such as worry, anger, resentment, fear, self-pity, and hopelessness slow down the movement of disease-fighting white cells and contribute to the development of stroke and heart disease by dumping high levels of adrenaline into the bloodstream. In other words, FEAR kills, FAITH heals.

We all need *Freedom from Fear* (the title of my first book, available at www.SparkingSuccess.net).

I am a true believer. Why? Five years ago, I was at death's door. Three days after my surgery in 2007 (I had a foot of my colon removed), I was not processing food. I was rushed back to the hospital a second time and the doctors removed my appendix and more of my colon. I should have died twice. During my recovery, I read up on this science of healing. I have made it a point to give thanks every day, aloud and on paper. I also made it a point to laugh every day. Moreover, I am on a mission to make other people laugh every day as well. *Laugh, Love, Learn, Leverage, and Leave a Legacy.* I have made the time every day since 2007 to live those five L's.

You cannot be grateful and unhappy at the same time. There are certain laws that operate whether we are aware of them or not. They are timeless laws, immutable principles that just are. Gratitude is one of those mysterious laws. The more gratitude we have, the more abundance we receive. The more cynical and ungrateful we are, the less we get. By becoming grateful, we set in motion a kind of magnet, attracting people, emotions, and attitudes that foster abundance. I don't completely understand it, but hey, I don't understand why my wife likes cut flowers. I buy them; they eventually die and are thrown away. However, I understand the effect. "Awww!" she exclaims. So I keep buying them. Gratitude is like that.

When you combine <u>gratitude</u> with <u>positive expectations</u>, something magic happens: You become an "Inverse Paranoid," someone who feels strongly that the world is out to *give* them! You become someone who believes the world is good. Great things just start happening. Great people show up in your life. Great days become the norm. So how do I foster an "Attitude of Gratitude"?

Begin by making a *Gratitude List.*

What are ten things (or people) for which (whom) you are grateful? Make your list now:

1). _____

2). _____

3). _____

4). _____

5). _____

6). _____

7). _____

8). _____

9). _____

10). _____

When you find yourself having a tough day, grab a pen and paper and make a list. What makes you smile? What is great about your life right now? It's impossible to be in the light and the darkness at the same time. They cannot coexist. When you focus on what you are grateful for, pessimism, cynicism, and negative attitudes disappear. You are transformed. I have made hundreds of these lists over the last thirty years. They are truly magical. Optimism will sneak up on you in the process. Guess what? Optimists live longer than pessimists do and they have a better time along the way. Appropriate, isn't it?

I don't have to chase extraordinary moments to find happiness—it's right in front of me. I only have to pay attention and practice gratitude to see it. So there it is. One day, shortly after my surgery, I wrote down a simple philosophy of life. I remind myself each day to remember to consciously do six things:

***Work Smart.***
***Be Kind.***
***Have Fun.***

**Keep Learning.**

**Help Others.**

**Give Thanks.**

*I try hard to hold fast to the truth that a full and thankful heart cannot entertain great conceits. When brimming with gratitude, ones heartbeat must surely result in outgoing love, the finest emotion that we can ever know.*

—Bill Wilson, co-founder of Alcoholics Anonymous

How about you? I'd love to hear from you . . .

**Your Ah-has? List Your Lights**

*"What is my philosophy?"*

_____

_____

_____

_____

_____

_____

_____

_____

_____

_____

_____

_____

## *Window Four*

# WHAT BOOKS DO YOU READ AND WHY?

*The Books you don't read won't help. People who don't read have no advantage over those who don't know how to read.* —Jim Rohn

**I'm writing this sitting on my deck** looking out over Puget Sound in lovely Edmonds, Washington. The sea is calm, the sky is an azure blue, and I have some extra time on my hands.

I've been on a not-so-secret mission to inspire my friends, family, and clients to read great books since 1990. If you have subscribed to my ezine since 2003, you know I profile a "Book of the Month." (For a FREE subscription to my e-newsletter, simply go to www.SparkingSuccess.net and click on the red SUB-SCRIBE NOW button). What qualifies me to make these suggestions? Simple. I read two books a week. I have for over thirty years. I'm not bragging. Hey, I'm the guy who had a year of junior college and flunked high school English! What I am saying is, after reading over 3,100 books for the last three decades in every genre—biographies, self-help, spiritual, history, business, sales, leadership, wellness, and nutrition—I have a unique perspective. For every ONE book on this list, there are FIVE that didn't make the cut. Every one of these books inspired me to take action, changed my awareness, lit a fire, gave me hope, and filled my mind with a unique perspective on life and business. The men and women who wrote these books spent years reading many more books than I ever did, and some of the best books ever written came out of the toughest times in U.S. history. Two of the books on the list, Dale Carnegie's *How to Win Friends and Influence People,* and Napoleon Hill's *Think and Grow Rich*, were written in the teeth of the Great Depression. Challenging times call for great minds to step up and offer solutions. We find ourselves in challenging times once again. Some of these books are all-time classics. They might not be on Oprah's list, but they will inspire and instruct you to take your game to the next level.

Oscar Wilde wrote, *"If one cannot enjoy reading a book over and over again, there is no use in reading it at all."*

Many of these books I have read more than once.

- ❑ 1) *Freedom from Fear*, by Mark Matteson
- ❑ 2) *Creative Visualization*, by Shakti Gawain
- ❑ 3) *Mindset*, by Carol Dweck
- ❑ 4) *Chop Wood Carry Water*, by Joshua Medcalf
- ❑ 5) *Think and Grow Rich*, by Napoleon Hill
- ❑ 6) *How to Win Friends and Influence People,* by Dale Carnegie
- ❑ 7) *Born to Run*, by Bruce Springsteen
- ❑ 8) *A Year of Living Kindly,* by Donna Cameron
- ❑ 9) *Born Standing Up*, by Steve Martin
- ❑ 10) *The Rise of Theodore Roosevelt,* by Edmund Morris
- ❑ 11) *Broken Music*, by Sting
- ❑ 12) *On Writing*, by Stephen King
- ❑ 13) *Body for Life*, by Bill Phillips

❏ 14) *It's About TIME*, by Mark Matteson

❏ 15) *The Culture Code*, by Daniel Coyle

❏ 16) *Good to Great*, by Jim Collins

❏ 17) *Mind Gym*, by Gary Mack

❏ 18) *Wooden on Leadership*, by John Wooden

❏ 19) *Atomic Habits*, by James Clear

❏ 20) *The Talent Code*, by Daniel Coyle

❏ 21) *Marketing Your Dreams*, by Pat Williams

❏ 22) *Unbroken*, by Laura Hillenbrand

❏ 23) *How to Raise Positive Kids in a Negative World,* by Zig Ziglar

❏ 24) *How to Sell Anything to Anybody*, by Joe Girard

❏ 25) *Learned Optimism*, by Martin Seligman

❏ 26) *Toughness*, by Jay Bilas

❏ 27) *Seven Spiritual Laws of Success*, by Deepak Chopra

❏ 28) *The Godfather*, by Mario Puzo

❏ 29) *The Unknown Lincoln*, by Dale Carnegie

❏ 30) *Freedom from Fear Forever*, by Mark Matteson

❏ 31) *Acres of Diamonds*, by Russell Conwell

❑ 32) *How to Read a Person Like a Book*, by Girard I. Nierenberg

❑ 33) *How to Deal with Nasty People*, by Jay Carter

❑ 34) *Moby-Dick*, by Herman Melville

❑ 35) *The History of the Decline and Fall of the Roman Empire*, by Edward Gibbon

❑ 36) *The Essays of Emerson,* by Ralph Waldo Emerson

❑ 37) *Of Mice and Men*, by John Steinbeck

❑ 38) *The Old Man and the Sea*, by Ernest Hemingway

❑ 39) *Hamlet*, by William Shakespeare

❑ 40) *A Tale of Two Cities,* by Charles Dickens

❑ 41) *Adventures of Huckleberry Finn*, by Mark Twain

❑ 42) *The Bible*

❑ 43) *The Picture of Dorian Gray*, by Oscar Wilde

❑ 44) *Robinson Crusoe*, by Daniel Defoe

❑ 45) *Pygmalion*, by George Bernard Shaw

❑ 46) *The Autobiography of Benjamin Franklin*, by Benjamin Franklin

❑ 47) *Aesop's Fables*

❑ 48) *Animal Farm*, by George Orwell

❑ 49) *Walden*, by Henry David Thoreau

❑ 50) *The Last of the Mohicans*, by James Fenimore Cooper

Will Rogers is one of my heroes. Although his biography didn't make the list, he had a unique and often hilarious perspective. He said, *"There are three kinds of men. The one that learns by reading. The few who learn by observation. The rest of them have to pee on the electric fence for themselves!"*

Ben Franklin advised, *"Either write something worth reading or do something worth writing about!"* If you are reading this, you are practicing "social distancing" and have some extra time on your hands. Why not choose a book from this list and read for twenty to thirty minutes a day? Your life will never be the same.

Now where did I put my copy of *Moby-Dick*? I just saw a whale in the harbor . . .

## Your Ah-has? List Your Lights

*"What books inspired me to change, grow, and become?"*

_____

_____

_____

_____

_____

_____

_____

_____

_____

_____

_____

_____

_____

_____

_____

_____

## *Window Five*

# FIND A NEED AND FILL IT

*The history of innovation is the story of ideas that seemed dumb at the time.* —Andy Dunn

**Tom Edison, Art Sill, and Bill Gates.** What do they have in common?

In February of 2000 I was delivering a Keynote in San Diego at the luxurious Hotel del Coronado. Built in 1888, the del Coronado is one of the country's most iconic hotels, with a rich and storied history (some claim it's haunted). I went to the weight room to work out and noticed a series of old photographs in the hallway featuring Tom Edison and his team installing the brand new "Electric Light System." There was a sign that served as both a precaution and comforting message: *"No harm will come to you by turning on this switch!"* You see, electricity was in its infancy. Why are we afraid of something new?

Edison and fellow electrical pioneer Nikola Tesla were locked in a historical race for market share. Edison had to *give away* the first few systems to create the demand and assure his customers it was safe and functional. Edison didn't just invent the light bulb. He had to build the entire system—from power plants to power poles, light bulbs, sockets, and switches. You get the idea. It was a massive undertaking. It worked. He created the demand. From then on, he was able to sell it to thousands of companies. He invented an industry. Tesla was left in the dust.

Russel Conwell, in his classic 1927 book *Acres of Diamonds*, posited, *"You live right in the middle of your own Acres of Diamonds. You must FIND A NEED AND FILL IT, FIRST OR BETTER!"*

Are you trying to sell new technology? Is it a breakthrough in its field?

Bill Gates and Paul Allen did essentially the same thing as Edison when they invented (or borrowed) software technology for PCs. They gave away the first version to create the demand for their new tech. Once the world was hooked, they upgraded the software to 2.0 and charged for it. The rest is history. Gates and Edison had that in common. Innovation is taking two things that already exist and putting them together in a new way.

*Every once in a while, a new technology and an old problem, along with a big idea, turn into an innovation!*
—Dean Kamen

*Success doesn't necessarily come from breakthrough innovation but from flawless execution. A great strategy alone won't win a game or a battle; the win comes from basic blocking and tackling.* —Naveen Jain

Selling new tech requires embracing a long term three-step process:

1)  Give away your product or service to establish value to create the demand (1.0).

2) Relentlessly update, upgrade, and improve your product or service and charge for the new technology (2.0).

3) Keep improving your product or service with extra-mile value and charge for the improvements (3.0).

Simple, not easy. It requires a tremendous amount of effort, patience, and time.

You might not have heard of Art Sill, but chances are you've used his invention many times. Art worked at 3M (Minnesota Mining and Manufacturing Company). He was in church one day singing in the choir. The pastor had told them which page the hymn was on, so Art marked the page with a slip of paper. He accidentally dropped the hymnal and the paper fell out. He was embarrassed, unable to find the page as the rest of the choir sang on without him.

Afterward, he presented himself with a challenge: *There must be a way to create a piece of paper that sticks to a page without tearing it, and can be used over and over again.* He began experimenting with different kinds of glue. With tremendous patience and persistence, the "Sticky Note" was born. But Art had a problem: *How do*

*I sell this idea and get people within 3M to use it and create the demand?* As the story goes, he asked the CEO's assistant if she could use his new sticky notes. He gave her a pad and said, "Tell me if you find it useful." A week later, she asked him if he had any more of those pads! The rest is history. Art invented an industry. He found a need and filled it, even though most people didn't even know the needed existed.

Isn't it fascinating that we take electricity, software, and sticky notes for granted today?

I need to get back to the Hotel del Coronado for a long weekend. I better bring some sticky notes and my computer. The lighting is so good. I need to get some work done . . .

## Your Ah-has? List Your Lights

*"What underserved needs exist within my industry?"*

_____

_____

_____

_____

_____

_____

_____

_____

_____

_____

_____

_____

_____

_____

_____

_____

_____

_____

_____

_____

_____

## *Window Six*

# IGNITION, BLAST OFF

*Successful people maintain a positive focus in life no matter what is going on around them. They stay focused on their past successes rather than their past failures, and on the next action steps they need to take to get them closer to the fulfillment of their goals rather than all the other distractions that life presents to them.* —Jack Canfield

**Where does inspiration come from?** Why does ignition burst and cause us to take action?

In 1991 I was in my second year in a sales job I loved. I was hungry. I had been a technician for ten years prior to that. My sales manager had suggested we read the trade magazines that circulated the office. One rainy

Saturday afternoon in Seattle, as I sat in my cubicle, it happened: Ignition, Blast Off! An article in *Contracting Business* profiled bestselling author, businessman and speaker Harvey Mackay. He had just written his first book, *How to Swim With the Sharks Without Being Eaten Alive.* The article profiled his typical week. Among his other activities, he read five hours a day, *every* day, magazines, newspapers, and, oh yes, books. Five hours! At the time I was reading maybe thirty minutes a day, primarily sales books. But the article was more than inspiration to read more. It became a kind of compass pointing north. I wanted to BE Harvey. I remember thinking, *If he can, maybe I could too . . . become an author and speaker. After all, he started as a lowly salesman. Why not me?* Then I chuckled to myself for thinking such an outrageous thought. But it was a rock in my shoe.

*If she can, so can I . . .* is what every young female golfer in South Korea said in 1998 when Se-ri Pak won the McDonald's LPGA Championship and became a national icon. One Seoul newspaper said, *"Se-ri Pak is not the female Tiger Woods, Tiger Woods is the male Se-ri Pak!"* Seemingly overnight, South Korea became a hotbed of talent for female golfers. Ten years after Se-ri Pak's success, forty-five South Korean female golfers collectively won a third of the events. It was an awakening, it was Ignition, Blast Off! *If SHE can, so can I!* the young golfing girls in South Korea affirmed and then took action.

This isn't a recent phenomenon. In 1954, a skinny Oxford medical student became the first person to run a mile in under four minutes. Physiologists and athletes believed the four-minute barrier was impossible to break. Yet after this guy broke the four-minute mile, within three years, seventeen other runners did it, too. It turns out it wasn't about positive thinking. The track hadn't changed. The training was the same. The change didn't come from the inside; those seventeen were inspired by an *outside change*. A paradigm shift. Ignition, Blast Off! It was an awakening. *If HE can, so can I!* Each of those runners said the same thing I said, and that all those young women in South Korea said: *If someone else can, why can't I?*

Fast forward twenty-five years. I have written six books and ten e-books. I conduct seventy-five talks a year around the globe. I am doing what Harvey Mackay inspired me to do all those years ago.

There were three simple steps to achieving my aim:

1)     Ignition (Blast Off!)
2)     Deep Practice (Reading Books Three Hours a Day)
3)     Master Coaching (Working for and Learning from Writing/Speaking Mentors)

Nelson Mandela said, *"There is no passion to be found playing small—in settling for a life that is less than the one you are capable of living."*

What inspired you in the past? What dream lies dormant in your heart and head? Begin searching outside yourself for that exemplar, that role model, that person who has done what you want to do and been where you want to go. *Unassertive people have skinny kids!* We must ask for what we want. Take a risk. Ask for help.

In 1997, six years after that magic Saturday, I made a list of all the books I had read that year. It was over a hundred. I sent that list to Harvey Mackay along with a heartfelt letter of appreciation for changing my direction and ultimately my destination. A week later, I received a three-page letter from him that said, *"Congratulations!"* 320 times, followed by *"Your reading accomplishments are nothing short of extraordinary! It's not IF you are*

***going to reach your goals, it's only WHEN! Keep up the good work!" —*Harvey Mackay**

I truly believe we all must find our *Ignition, Blast Off* that inspires us to take action with Deep Practice that leads inevitably to Master Coaching. In the end, it's what we DO that follows our ignition that determines our success. A little coaching doesn't hurt. Thanks, Harvey. I love "Swimming with The Sharks!!"

## Your Ah-has? List Your Lights

*"Who has inspired me?"*

_____

_____

_____

_____

_____

_____

_____

_____

_____

_____

_____

_____

_____

_____

_____

_____

# DEEP PRACTICE

*The sweet spot: that productive, uncomfortable terrain located just beyond our current abilities, where our reach exceeds our grasp. Deep practice is not simply about struggling; it's about seeking a particular struggle, which involves a cycle of distinct actions.* —Daniel Coyle, Author of *The Talent Code*

**Vladimir Horowitz,** the virtuoso pianist, was once asked by a reporter why, in his eighties, he still practiced three hours a day. *"If I skip one day, I notice. If I skip two days, my wife notices. If I skip three days, the world notices!"*

Every day I read fifty pages from a book aligned with my number-one goal. I write three pages a day, every

day. It's a habit. Aristotle said, *"Excellence is a habit."*
First we form habits, then they form us. Good habits are
hard to form but easy to live with. Bad habits are easy to
form and hard to live with.

One sunny October, fifteen years ago in Cincin-
nati, Ohio, at Cintas Arena, I watched my old friend, John
Lucas (New Jersey Nets coach at the time) rebound for
Nick Van Exel. It was very focused, very deliberate, very
intense. For thirty minutes, Nick ran to each spot as John
whipped passes to him and Nick drained it. Afterwards, I
asked the NBA legend exactly what he was doing. "Oh, I
call it *5-Shots-From-5-Spots.* I insist all my guys do it
every day. You see, eighty percent of the shots a player
takes, if you examine a game's shot chart, come from five
spots on the floor." He had his players engage in *Deep
Practice*, a term Daniel Coyle coined in his seminal book
*The Talent Code.*

Have you heard of Ray LaMontagne? His 2008
LP *Gossip in the Grain*, and specifically the song "You
Are the Best Thing," simply blew me away. At age
twenty-two, Ray had an epiphany. At the time, he was an
unhappy worker at a shoe factory in Lewiston, Maine, a
town of 36,000 people. He decided to become a singer-

songwriter. With little musical experience and even less money, he took a simple approach to learning how to sing. He bought dozens of used albums by Stephen Stills, Ray Charles, Otis Redding, Al Green, and Etta James and holed up in his apartment. For two years, every day, for hours at a time, he trained himself by singing along to the records. His friends assumed he left town. His coworkers thought him insane. He locked himself in a kind of musical time capsule. He said, "I would sing and sing and hurt and hurt, because I knew I wasn't doing it right. It took a long time. I finally learned how to sing from the gut." Eight years after he started, his first album sold over half a million copies. The main reason was his soulful voice and thoughtful lyrics. *Rolling Stone* magazine wrote, *"He sounds like church."* If you listen to his music, he does. He used imitation and deep practice to hone his skills.

What are doing to work on your skills? What good habits are you forming? Whether you are a manager, a salesperson, a teacher, a doctor, or an engineer, how committed are you to *Deep Practice?* What are you doing EVERY DAY to hone your skills?

Deep Practice is starting and stopping. It's failing forward. It's doing it wrong and adjusting. It's investing your time and effort on all the little things. The talent comes from focused effort and hard, time-consuming work. It's **R.E.T.**—**R**epetition + **E**motion + **T**ime = Skill. It's persistence combined with consistent effort to achieve mastery.

Mr. Horowitz was right. If you skip a day, YOU will notice. If you skip two days, your SPOUSE will notice. If you skip three days, the WORLD will notice! Excellence IS a habit.

Now what did I do with my dogeared copy of *The Talent Code?* I have got to read fifty pages today . . .

## Your Ah-has? List Your Lights

*"What skills am I developing with deep practice?"*

_____

_____

_____

_____

_____

_____

_____

_____

_____

_____

_____

_____

_____

_____

_____

_____

_____

## *Window Eight*

# WHO ARE YOUR MENTORS?

*Find a great mentor who believes in you; your life will change forever!* —Bill Walsh, NFL Coach, San Francisco 49ers, three-time Super Bowl champion

**As I mentioned previously,** my first real inspirational mentor was Bob Moawad. He taught high school psychology and coached boy's basketball at Central Kitsap High in the 1960s where he won a state championship. At the time, Lou Tice, who had formerly been a state championship football coach turned public speaker, hired Bob to be on his staff. In 1971, Lou's company was The Pacific Institute and their primary audience was coaches, teachers, and student athletes. Bob offered a two-day seminar entitled *Action for Excellence* for forty-five dollars! School assemblies were how Bob marketed his seminars, and I was hooked at fourteen years of age. I convinced my mother to drive me to Seattle University on Super Bowl Weekend in 1971. I took fifty pages of notes and learned how to set goals, understand the value of self-talk, self-esteem, self-worth, attitude, and visualization. I took to it like a duck to water and I went from scrub to star in basketball in three weeks! Shifting my focus to academics, I went from a 1.8 GPA to a 3.8 GPA in one quarter using Bob's Goal Achievement Process!

Eventually, Bob Moawad shifted his client focus from teachers to business professionals. We reunited in 1993 and he recruited me to work for him. I was the top salesman in my company at the time (selling commercial HVAC service agreements, a complex and difficult sale). I worked for Bob at Edge Learning Institute in Tacoma for almost four years, then I went out on my own and have never looked back.

I met Charlie "Tremendous" Jones by way of his audio tape program. Bob Moawad had hundreds of audio programs and I had a fifty-five-mile, one-way commute each day. I devoured them all in my daily three-hour commute; I called it *Windshield University*. I reached out to

Mr. Jones and he became my next mentor who eventually taught me the book business. He published my first four books. It was a win-win relationship up until his death in 2008. Now I'm a publisher.

I am a solo entrepreneur with no employees. I do it all myself (sales, marketing, writing, speaking, billing, etc.). I use Amazon's Kindle Direct publishing system and manage my own inventory. Every one of my speaking engagement offers several options that include books. I just closed a deal that included 8,000 books—and I was paid in advance!

My point? *What one man or woman can do, another can!*

Birds of a feather flock together. Emerson said, "If we are related, we shall meet!"

A word of advice when seeking out mentors: DO NOT simply call someone and ask to "Pick their brain." You are asking a super busy and successful person to give a stranger something for nothing. I offered to pick Charlie Jones up at his hotel and drive him to his gig. He said yes. I attended Dan Poynter's seminars three times (he wrote

120 books!) and offered to get him lunch so he could keep selling and signing books. A couple of years later I hired him to coach me for an hour at five hundred dollars to teach me to market my books. Best money I ever spent. Learn to be a Go-Giver, not a Go-Taker.

Respect the other person's time. What can *you* give?

I'm grateful to Bob, Charlie, and Dan. They were life-changing mentors—master coaches. May they rest in peace.

## Your Ah-has? List Your Lights

*"Who are my mentors? How do they inspire me?"*

_____

_____

_____

_____

_____

_____

_____

_____

_____

_____

_____

_____

_____

_____

_____

_____

## *Window Nine*

# ARE YOU IN THE C.I.A.?

*You can make more friends in two minutes by becoming genuinely interested in other people—than you can in two years by trying to get other people interested in you.*
—Dale Carnegie, *How to Win Friends and Influence People*

**I was speaking in Las Vegas recently** and had the pleasure of seeing a presentation by Max Major, a magician and mentalist. He was extraordinary. The illusions, his fluid, often hilarious "Magic" was over-the-top, knock-your-socks-off amazing. He used an example of how to build rapport with strangers by communicating a simple three-step formula:

1)  **Compliment**
2)  **Introduce**
3)  **Ask**

As he explained the process, I thought, Wait a minute . . . *I've been doing this for YEARS!* As I jotted down the formula, it hit me: I'll create a simple acronym to remember it. I'll call it *C.I.A.*

Here's an example of this system in action, in my own words:

**Compliment**
I always arrive at least an hour before presenting a keynote or seminar. Invariably, an early bird will show up thirty to forty-five minutes beforehand. If it's a man in his fifties or sixties, with an impressive head of hair (because I don't have one!) I'll approach him and say, *"You have waaaay too much hair for a guy your age!"* They always smile. Sometimes, they tell me a story. It always elicits a positive response.

## Introduction

I follow that up with, *"Good morning! Mark Matteson (as I reach my hand out to shake his). I'm the speaker today. I'm so glad you came. And your name is?"*

## Ask

Now I have a real connection with a former stranger. If he's with his wife, I'll ask, *"How did you two meet?"* If he's alone, I'll say, *"So where did you come in from?"* followed closely by, *"So what do you for the company?"* Then I listen actively, smiling, leaning forward, nodding, and occasionally paraphrasing. It never fails, they always appreciate my approach. I made a friend. The whole process takes a minute or two.

Everyone you meet is looking for three things: *Appreciation, Respect, and Understanding.*

Mary Kay Ash, who built a billion-dollar cosmetics business, used to tell her sales professionals, *"Ladies, every woman you meet has a stamp on her forehead that says, 'Make me feel important!' So let's do that with every woman you meet and then sell her the makeup to cover it up!"*

Is it time to adopt this habit with everyone you meet? It's so simple.

Why not join the C.I.A.? You don't have to be Jack Ryan to make this happen! You can make more friends in two minutes by being genuinely interested in them than trying for two years to get them interested in you. If you want to be interesting to others, be interested in them first and always!

I need to send Max Major a thank you note. He reminded me how important it is to build rapport and influence others by being other-centered.

It's not magic. It's just un-common sense!

## Your Ah-has? List Your Lights

*"Why not join the C.I.A.?"*

_____

_____

_____

_____

_____

_____

_____

_____

_____

_____

_____

_____

_____

_____

_____

_____

_____

_____

_____

# Window Ten

## WHAT THE ... ?

*To forgive is to set a prisoner free and discover that the prisoner was you.* —Lewis B. Smedes, author of *Forgive and Forget*

**My parents met in 1949** at South Ruislip Air Station just outside of London. My father was in the US Air Force. One sunny day in July he was playing in a softball game as the catcher. This was odd, as the year before he was *pitching* for the Dayton Mudhens, a AA professional baseball team in Ohio. The softball game was just a bit of fun. As the story goes, he spied a lovely girl through his mask and at the end of the inning he asked his friend in the dugout who that girl was. "Oh, that's Jean. She's my girlfriend's best friend. Would you like to meet her?" That is how it began.

My father was a strapping twenty-year-old, standing six-foot-four with 220 pounds of muscle, wavy black hair, and an infectious smile and a delightful sense of humor. My mother, maybe five-foot-five in heels and wore her red hair in a fashionable 1940s style. She was purportedly a fine dancer, very smart for her age (seventeen), and a little bit shy. Their first date was to Eel Island, a famous and very popular dance hall. (It's where a sixteen-year-old busker by the name of Rod Stewart would be discovered and asked to join Long John Baldry's skiffle band. My mother's first cousin, Cyril Davies, had started the band and was considered by most musicians to be the finest blues harmonica player in the U.K. Sadly, he died at age thirty-one, and that's when Mr. Baldry took over the band). But I digress.

My future parents hit it off and were soon a couple. Young lovers. Six weeks later they were married. They had big plans. They both worked hard, saving half of their income over the next two years, diligently mailing money home to Ravenna, Ohio to my father's mother, Electa Matteson, to build a nest egg for their new family.

My mother was pregnant with my brother Bruce. My mother's Mum also added money to the pot.

After two years, the money sent and saved was a sizable amount. My father was eventually deployed back home to Ohio. Upon arriving home, he went to the bank to make a withdrawal only find to his shock and astonishment that ALL THE MONEY WAS GONE! His mother, a low-bottom alcoholic, had drank it all away. Gone. What the . . . ?

This unconscionable act of betrayal and selfishness, that only an alcoholic is capable of, sent my parents reeling. With a newborn baby, no money, and a bitter and strained relationship with his mother, my parents shifted gears and went to work. My father took a thirty-day leave (his vacation days) from the Air Force and worked two jobs: During the day he laid asphalt and at night he tended bar.

A month later he got his orders to Yokohama, Japan. They left with their heads held high, not owing a cent to anyone. He would never speak to his mother again. I only saw him cry once. I was eleven. The phone call came one night: His mother had passed away. In retrospect, I believe they were tears of regret for an abusive childhood and love lost.

It's been said, *Adversity doesn't make the man, it reveals him to himself.*

I learned this story in my twenties, after our first son was born. It gave me a tremendous amount of respect for my parents. They stayed married for over fifty-five years and built a wonderful life for themselves and their family.

When I was twenty-two my wife and I bought the house I grew up in from my parents. When I was a child I never wanted for anything. My parents gave me the gift of hard work. Through courageous attitude and able example, my wife and I gave that same gift to our children.

My parents also taught me *It's not what happens, rather it's how we respond to setbacks, challenges, frustrations, and betrayal.* I am proud of my parents. I miss them every day. It's not how you start but how you finish. I don't know if my father ever really forgave his mother. I guess I'll never know.

Lewis B. Smedes wrote in his book *Forgive and Forget*, "*Forgiving does not erase the bitter past. A healed memory is not a deleted memory. Instead, forgiving what we cannot forget creates a new way to remember. We change the memory of our past into a hope for our future.*"

I'd like to believe that's what my parents did. They changed the memory of their past into a hope for the future. That is all any of us can do. Forgive and forget. Or maybe, *forgive and remember the lesson,* so we don't pass that betrayal on to the next generation.

Thanks Mum and Dad . . . I miss you every day.

## Your Ah-has? List Your Lights

*"Whom do I need to forgive?"*

_____

_____

_____

_____

_____

_____

_____

_____

_____

_____

_____

_____

_____

_____

_____

_____

_____

_____

_____

_____

## WHY I WRITE

*Window Eleven*

*If you want to be a writer, you must do two things above all others: read a lot and write a lot. There's no way around those two things . . .* —Stephen King, bestselling author, icon

**I write three pages every day** when I am not traveling. That's 150 days a year which, multiplied by three, is 450 pages a year. Some of it ends up as an article for a magazine, others a special report, or a chapter in a book, or an e-book. Sometimes what I write just sits in a file—like an apple in a bowl waiting to be eaten.

So why do I write?

I write to learn.

I write to process.

I write to examine.

I write to understand my past.

I write to reinforce a belief.

I write to remember.

I write to create.

I write to clarify.

I write to inspire myself and others.

I write to heal.

I write to affirm what I believe.

I write to clear my head.

I write to get it all out on paper.

I write to honor my past.

I write to write . . . because that is what writers do. They write.

I am a writer.

The creative process demands consistency. It's a habit. Like breathing, writing is central to my being. It's a part of who I am. I could no more not write than not eat. Writing is a muscle that gets bigger and stronger with use. It expands my vocabulary. It feeds my soul. It gives voice to the ideas floating around my head so I can make sense of it all.

I live two lives. As a professional speaker, facilitator, consultant, and coach, that part of me lives in the limelight. The stage is the place I share ideas on transformation, information, lessons, insights, mistakes, humor, inspiring stories, and best practices. It's a platform from which I deliver the things I have been learning in an effort to assist the audience to achieve their goals. It's very public. I am a *situational extrovert*. Some people call it an *ambivert*. Whatever it is, it began when I was five years old. When I have an audience, something changes inside of me. When I am "ON," whether that's entertaining a barista at a coffee shop, or the teller at the bank, or my travel agent, it is spontaneous. Sometimes I test new material. Sometimes it's just to see if I can make someone laugh, cry, or think. My older brother used to say to me when I was eight or nine years old, "If you don't talk for twenty minutes I will give you a quarter!" I never got the money.

Writing is very private. It's the other part of my personality. The other side of my coin, the tails to my heads. Because I read at least fifty pages a day from books, all kinds of books—spiritual, business, wellness, fiction, biographies/memoirs, self-help, psychology—it all blends together like a kind of eclectic stew. Perhaps it's more like a pond: the water comes in; it must at some point go out. For all the reasons listed above and more, I write. I will do so until they (whoever they might be) pry my cold dead fingers from my laptop. Writers live longer than most people for one simple reason: *They never retire!* There is always one more story to write.

I flunked high school English. I have a year of junior college. It turns out, writing has nothing to do with English. *Thank God.* One day, in my mid-twenties, I decided to become a writer. That decision gave my life purpose, meaning, and structure.

*The road to hell is paved with adverbs.* —Stephen King

*Cheat your landlord if you can and must, but do not try to shortchange the Muse. It cannot be done. You can't fake quality any more than you can fake a good meal.* —William S. Burroughs

*Who wants to become a writer? And why? Because it's the answer to everything—It's the streaming reason for*

*living. To note, to pin down, to build up, to create, to be astonished at nothing, to cherish the oddities, to let nothing go down the drain, to make something, to make a great flower out of life, even if it's a cactus.* —Enid Bagnold

Now you know why I write.

## Your Ah-has? List Your Lights

*"Why do I do what I do?"*

_____

_____

_____

_____

_____

_____

_____

_____

_____

_____

_____

_____

_____

_____

_____

_____

_____

_____

*Window Twelve*

# GHOSTS OR ANCESTORS? (THEY ARE NEVER REALLY GONE)

*Ghosts or ancestors? Which one will you be?*
—Bruce Springsteen

**Today is my 63rd Birthday.** I am in a contemplative mood. I find myself thinking about my parents. Dad passed away in 2005, Mum in 2010.

Recently I was sitting in the Delta Lounge at SeaTac airport listening to a song by Mike Posner. He was singing about his parents: *"They are never really gone . . . "* It got me thinking. As I write this, I'm drinking a cup of tea, Tetley's. It's an English brand. It's what "Me Mum" drank. She was very British. I have one or two cups every day. Why? Mum did. I'm a funny guy. How do I know? People laugh (with me) when I tell a story. I don't tell jokes. I tell humorous stories with a twist at the end. My father loved telling stories. He was fond of bad puns. He would sit back with a self-satisfied grin after making someone laugh. I do that. But my stories are much funnier than my dad's (sorry, Pop!). Mum and Dad are inside me. Mum and Dad are inside my boys . . .

I have a picture of my father wearing a #13 tank-top jersey and short shorts, basketball gear circa 1950. He is posing. The ball rests on the palm of his hand and he looks up to an imaginary hoop, as if he's about to release the shot. It's a profile. If I put our youngest son Evan in the same pose, you would think they were the same person. It's uncanny. My father played basketball in Germany, as did our oldest son Colin. Hmmmm . . .

My father grew up during the (not so Great) Depression. He used to say, "Waste not, want not!" Regardless of what we ate the night before, he would say, concerning the fate of the leftovers, "No, don't throw that out, I'll eat it for breakfast in the morning." And he did. Every time. He would stand, eating it over the sink, looking out into the back yard, searching for future chores for me.

There isn't a day that goes by, especially now that I'm sixty-three years young, that I don't think about my parents. They loved their family. They were survivors. They did it all together, through thick and thin (and there was a lot of thin!).

Growing up, if I wanted something—a new bicycle, a mini-bike, a car—the answer was always the same: "You earn half, we will pay the other half." And they did. Mum would often say, "Take all you want, but eat all you take!" When I didn't finish my meal, they would say, "Your eyes were bigger than your belly!" Have a nice guilt trip.

I am grateful for my childhood, for my late parents, for my siblings, for my boys, for my grandchildren. Writing about my youth helps me understand the man I have become.

One day, after I'm gone, my boys will say, "My dad used to say . . ." or "My dad loved basketball . . ." or "I miss my dad, it was his birthday today."

It's true. WE are never really gone . . . we just move on. But we all leave a legacy, positive or negative. Able example or cautionary tale?

Bruce Springsteen said in his heartfelt hit, *Springsteen on Broadway:*

*We are ghosts or we are ancestors in our children's lives. We either lay our mistakes and our burdens upon them, and we haunt them as ghosts. Or, we assist them in laying those old burdens down, and we free them from the chains of our own flawed behavior, and as ancestors, we walk alongside of them, assisting them to find their own way, and some sense of transcendence.*

I know what you must be thinking: "Take parenting advice from rock stars?" But he asks a great question. Ghosts or ancestors? Which will I be? Which will *you* be?

## Your Ah-has? List Your Lights

*"Which will I be, a ghost or an ancestor?"*

_____

_____

_____

_____

_____

_____

_____

_____

_____

_____

_____

_____

_____

_____

_____

_____

_____

_____

## Window Thirteen

# WHAT A DIFFERENCE A DAY MAKES

*Music is probably the only real magic I have encoun-
tered in my life. There's not some trick involved with it.
It's pure and it's real. It moves, it heals, it communicates and does all these incredible things.* —Tom Petty

**Stanley Adams was an American lyricist** and songwriter. He wrote the English lyrics for the song "What a
Difference a Day Makes." Adams was the president of the
American Society of Composers, Authors and Publishers
between 1953 and 1956, and again from 1959 until 1980.

*What a difference a day makes
Twenty-four little hours,
Brought the sun and the flowers
Where there used to be rain*

We all have bad days filled with challenges, setbacks, frustrations, resentments, and fear. No matter what is going in our life, a divorce, a death in the family, a layoff from our job, or an argument with a neighbor or friend, remember what Colin Powell said: *"Things always look different in the morning."*

Groucho Marx once said, *"Time wounds all heels."* I love that. In a single clever mnemonic, he gives us the answer. TIME. Time and tide wash away the pain. No matter what is happening in my life, I make it a point to remind myself that every bad thing that happens is temporary. In every dark cloud there is a silver lining.

What follows are simple strategies to navigate the rapids of change, that allows me to let the river do the work, and to appreciate the froth and foam of the currents.

1)  Write it out. Keep a journal. Describe the challenge or situation in detail along with possible solutions. Writing gives us distance and perspective.

2)  Ask myself, "What is GREAT about this?" and "What am I learning from all this?" and "What will I do differently next time this happens?"

3) Talk it over with someone I respect; a community of like-minded people, a coach, mentor, Dutch uncle. Get some objectivity.

4) Prayer is talking to God.

5) Meditation is listening for the answers.

6) Go for a walk, run, yoga, swim. Get out of the office or house.

7) Do something nice for someone else. Get out of myself.

Will these ideas fix everything? Maybe not. But any or all them will change the way we look at things. *When we change the way we look at things, the things we look at change.* Action and time will relieve us from our moribund mindset and become harbingers of hope.

Cause, effect. Reap, sow.

I am fond of Rod Stewart's version of "What a Difference a Day Makes." Listen here:

https://bit.ly/3wCE16f

Stanley Adams had it right, "24 little hours . . ."

## Your Ah-has? List Your Lights

*"Will I feel the same way tomorrow morning?"*

_____

_____

_____

_____

_____

_____

_____

_____

_____

_____

_____

_____

_____

_____

_____

_____

_____

_____

_____

_____

_____

## *Window Fourteen*

# WANTED: DEAD OR ALIVE

*People are always asking me why they don't make Westerns like they used to.* —Roy Rogers

**I've always loved Westerns.** My first mentor was Roy Rogers. As a kid growing up on an air force base in Japan, I went to the movies every Saturday to see my hero on his horse, Trigger, and his dog Bullet win the day and defeat the bad guys. In almost every Western, a poster would proclaim "WANTED DEAD OR ALIVE . . . ."

My speaking and writing mentors fall into two categories, DEAD or ALIVE. I discovered Earl Nightingale a year after he died, in 1989. He had done what I wanted to do and been where I wanted to go. He was an inspiring speaker and a gifted writer. His radio show *Our Changing World* was heard in over fifty countries. There was something about him, his voice, his vocabulary, his content, his positive point of view. I modeled my career after his. He said, *"Learn to enjoy every minute of your life. Be happy now. Don't wait for something outside of yourself to make you happy in the future. Think how really precious is the time you have to spend, whether it's at work or with your family. Every minute should be enjoyed and savored."*

A mentor does not need to be living to inspire and instruct. To wit: Teddy Roosevelt, George Bernard Shaw, Jim Rohn, Vince Lombardi, John Wooden, Dale Carnegie, Napoleon Hill, Bob Moawad, Charlie Jones, and Bill Wilson are all alive and well in my heart and head in the legacy they left behind. They continue to teach through their books, audios, videos, articles, and films. They left behind a shade tree I get to sit under and enjoy. In choosing my mentors, I ask a few simple questions:

1) Who has done what I want to do and been where I want go?

2) Who were my mentors coming up?

3) What books should I read?

4)   What YouTube Videos or TED Talks should I watch?

5)   What audio programs should I listen to?

I keep my journal handy and capture the answers to the questions "What are the causes of their success?" and "What can I borrow from them?"

Robert Klein is one of my comedy mentors. I read his book. I've seen him live several times. I watched interviews with him on YouTube. I downloaded his LP on iTunes. I deconstructed his style, use of accents and imitations, timing, pace, stories, and admired his extraordinary gift on the harmonica. Rodney Dangerfield said in 1966, *"Robert Klein is the new dimension in comedy,"* then proceeded to take the young man under his wing for ten years. (Rodney did the same thing for Jim Carrey. He had a keen eye for talent!). Jerry Seinfeld said, *"He was my first mentor, he changed my life and made me want to be a comedian!"* When Jay Leno was young he had a poster of Klein in his apartment.

That's what mentors do. They change our lives. They make us want to be better, DEAD or ALIVE!

As Roy Rogers said, *"I did pretty good for a guy who never finished high school and used to yodel at square dances!"*

Giddy up!

## Your Ah-has? List Your Lights

*"Who are my dead mentors?"*

_____

_____

_____

_____

_____

_____

_____

_____

_____

_____

_____

_____

_____

_____

_____

_____

_____

## *Window Fifteen*

# DO YOU TAKE A LOT OF PICTURES?

*You don't make a photograph just with a camera. You bring to the act of photography all the pictures you have seen, the books you have read, the music you have heard, the people you have loved.* —Ansel Adams, photographer

**Pictures are a moment in time.** It's amazing, really, how fast time flies. Like a roll of toilet paper, it goes faster the closer we get to the end. I have a lovely picture of the family from twenty-four years ago. As I examine it I realize that Evan was five and Colin was nine. My parents are gone. My nephew Adrian is married with a little baby boy, Malcom. My brother-in-law Bert is completely grey and I am bald (okay, I shave my head but let's be honest: like my old man, there ain't much snow on the roof!)

Why are pictures so important to us? When my children come over to our place, they look through a stack of pictures, in the selfsame way I used to pore over family scrapbooks when I visited my parents' place. *Home is where our history is.* Pictures are frozen moods, temporary slivers of memories, warm fuzzy feelings of *connections.* Like sand passing through an hourglass, ever changing. They represent connection, meaning, belonging, safety, and bonds to our distant past.

I recall with great affection my father saying to me one day when I was around eleven years old, *"Do what I SAY, not what I DO!"* I remember thinking, *That is such crap.* I never listened to what my parents said, but I *watched* every move they made.

When I was a new parent, I stumbled on a little book by Wilferd Peterson entitled *The Art of Living.* He offered some advice on parenting that I have never forgotten . . .

*"Of all the commentaries on the Scriptures,"* wrote John Donne, *"good examples are the best." In practicing the art of parenthood, an ounce of example is worth a ton of*

*preachment. Our children are watching us live, and what we ARE shouts louder than anything we can SAY.*

*Don't just stand there pointing your finger to the heights you want your children to scale. Start climbing, and they will follow!*

I am proud of the men my boys have become. They are quite simply the best thing I ever made (okay, so my wife helped . . .). Parenting is hard. When they are babies it seems they will never be out of diapers. Will we ever get a good night's sleep? As they get older, we complain about driving them hither and yon. One day, we wake up and *they* are driving, and then, in the blink of an eye, they are off to college. Now? They are having children of their own. We think they're not getting any of the things we try to teach. Out of the blue, they astonish us with their maturity, insight, and wisdom. One day, after some feedback about my childish behavior being called onto the carpet, it dawned on me: *They are never too young to teach; and I'm never too old to learn.* The son had become the father. Huh!?

Our oldest son Colin and his lovely wife Claire have two amazing girls; Penelope will be five soon,

Sawyer just turned eighteen months. Being a father of girls has transformed my son into a loving, caring, doting, kind, and patient dad. He realizes the men his daughters will eventually marry are going to be mirror images of him. Evan and Gen are expecting a boy in May! It's true, we become our parents, good or bad, positive or negative. Most of the time, it's a blend of the two. Thankfully, my boys have adopted most of the best qualities of my wife and I—and almost none of the bad.

This weekend my family is meeting up to camp at Birch Bay, Washington. We'll take lots of pictures (and videos with our iPhones). They will be treasured moments in time. I can't wait . . .

Pictures really are precious moments in time.

## Your Ah-has? List Your Lights

*"Do I have a scrapbook of fond memories?"*

_____

_____

_____

_____

_____

_____

_____

_____

_____

_____

_____

_____

_____

_____

_____

_____

_____

_____

_____

_____

# Window Sixteen

# THE JOY OF TRAVEL

*Nothing so liberalizes a man and expands the kindly instincts that nature put in him as travel and contact with many kinds of people.* —Mark Twain

**I have been traveling every week** for over twenty-five years as a professional speaker. I love what I do. When I tell people about my schedule they often look at me like I have two heads coming out of my neck. More than once I've heard someone say, "Oh, do you HAVE to travel? That must be hard . . ." I smile, pause for effect, and then say, "I GET to travel. It's a joy. I love every part of the process. Packing, driving to the airport, waiting for my flight, reading a good book, watching a movie, writing. Life at thirty thousand feet is amazing!"

To put it in perspective, my mother was a travel agent. She was born and raised in England. All her relatives were there. Even though I wasn't raised in affluence, flying to England every other summer from 1965 to 1975 was a priority to "me mum." I thought it was normal. Moreover, we moved to Japan when I was two years old and was raised by Yosh-Ko-San. Little boys in Japan were spoiled rotten back then.

I have worked in forty-seven states and on three continents. The first time I went to Australia a women raised her eyebrows and asked about the length of the flight. "Oh, it's a little over fourteen hours from LA to Sydney." She was astonished. Again, I smiled, paused, and replied, "It's all in how you look at it. It's a novel, three movies, two naps, and a couple of meals. Then, abracadabra, you are *down under*. I love it!"

What follows is the short list of some of the things I've seen and places I've been. To quote Dr. Suess, *"Oh the places you'll go . . ."*

- ❑ The Sydney Opera House, Australia
- ❑ The River Walk on the Yarra River in Melbourne, Australia

- Hagia Sophia, Topkapi Palace, The Blue Mosque, Sultanahmet Square, and of course The Grand Bazaar (the first and one of the largest malls in the world!) in Istanbul, Turkey
- Eagle Beach in Aruba
- Puerto Vallarta, Mazatlán, Cabo San Lucas, Mexico
- The Alamo in San Antonio, Texas (3x)
- Albuquerque, New Mexico (5x) Taking the tram to the top of the mountain is a must!
- Denver, Colorado (3x) Once watching a Colorado Rockies MLB game!
- Watching the New England Patriots vs. Carolina Cougars in the snow ("Mahk, It's Wicked Cold Out Heer!")
- Charlotte, Gastonia, Southern Pines, Raleigh, North Carolina (3x)
- Boston (3x) including a Red Sox game at Fenway Park (The most expensive and worst hot dog I ever had; hey I was warned!)
- Madison Square Garden to watch the Knicks play (Spike Lee wasn't there)
- New York City: The Empire State Building, the original World Trade Center, a horse-and-buggy

ride with my wife in Central Park, Broadway to see *The Producers* with Mathew Broderick and Nathan Lane, and a slice at Ray's Pizza

❑ Fond du Lac, Appleton, Madison, Milwaukee (3x), Wisconsin (it was two degrees!)

❑ Fairbanks and Anchorage, Alaska (6x)

❑ Hawaii (Maui 2x, The Big Island 5x, Kona 2x, Oahu 7x)

❑ Scottsdale, Tempe, Yuma, Arizona (12x)

❑ Detroit Country Club, Yacht Club, Detroit Tigers Game

❑ Texas Rangers, Chicago White Sox, Baltimore Orioles to watch the Mariners lose (sigh . . .)

❑ Fifteen NBA Games in various cities around the country

❑ Lake Champlain, Vermont

❑ Ben and Jerry's in Stowe, Vermont

❑ Myrtle Beach, South Carolina (2x) It's so warm

❑ Virtually every big city in Florida multiple times

❑ Norman, Oklahoma (10x)

❑ Nashville, Tennessee (5x) including speaking at the Country Music Hall of Fame and Gaylord Hotel (3x)

- ❑ Memphis, Tennessee (3x) (Graceland, home of Elvis; the Jungle Room is a must see!)
- ❑ Watching the St. Louis Cardinals play (2x) I've never seen so much red.
- ❑ Having a Dodger Dog in LA sitting behind the third-base dugout
- ❑ My hero Teddy Roosevelt's house on Long Island
- ❑ Mark Twain's house in Connecticut
- ❑ Powell's Books in Portland, Oregon
- ❑ The Magic Castle in Los Angeles
- ❑ The San Diego Zoo and Hotel del Coronado (3x)
- ❑ Played basketball in Venice Beach, California
- ❑ The Wharf and Coit Tower in San Francisco
- ❑ The Broadmoor in Colorado (3x) The finest hotel in the country!
- ❑ Boise State University (above the Blue Field)
- ❑ Laredo, Texas (7x) Our youngest son Evan was an All-American in Basketball at Texas A&M International
- ❑ University of Louisville (4x) (Including sitting in the coach's boat as the Women's Crew cut through the water in a synchronized display of athleticism and teamwork. Amazing!)

- ❑ Lexington, Kentucky (2x) (Got a private tour of Rupp Arena)
- ❑ Spokane, Washington (15x)
- ❑ Yakima, Washington (8x)
- ❑ Las Vegas, Nevada (7x) staying in every major resort/casino
- ❑ Salt Lake City, Park City, Utah (Where I had dinner with the guys who wrote and recorded "Louie Louie")
- ❑ The Stanley Hotel, Colorado (Haunted!)
- ❑ Whitefish, Butte, Great Falls, Conrad, and Billings, Montana
- ❑ Wichita, Kansas (2x)
- ❑ Lincoln, Nebraska (the home of Johnny Carson)
- ❑ Fort Smith, Arkansas (3x) (The airport lobby has dozens of comfy overstuffed mancave chairs)
- ❑ Cedar Rapids, Iowa (3x)
- ❑ Joliet, Illinois (2x) (home of Richard Pryor)
- ❑ Deadwood, Wall, Sioux Falls, and Rapid City, South Dakota (5x) On one occasion, speaking to 1,300 people!
- ❑ Fargo, North Dakota (2x) It's actually very nice . . .

- ❑ Soaring Eagle Casino (3x) in Central Michigan
- ❑ Chicago, Illinois (20x!) What can I say, they love me in the Windy City! The Sears Tower, Blue Man Group, The Second City
- ❑ New Orleans, Louisiana (The Big Easy) (4x)
- ❑ Atlanta (3x) and Augusta, Georgia (I had my picture taken with my arm around the James Brown Statue!)
- ❑ Cleveland, Ohio (3x) Including going to an Indians game with my cousin Kip Matteson and the Rock and Roll Hall of Fame
- ❑ Niagara Falls, Canada (2x) Amazing!
- ❑ Virginia (is for Lovers) at least five cities
- ❑ Philly, The City of Brotherly Love (5x) Oh those Philly cheesesteaks wit Whiz!
- ❑ Morgantown, West Virginia (Home of Jerry West)
- ❑ Montgomery, Alabama (Roll Tide)
- ❑ Phoenix, Arizona (watched the Suns play three times)
- ❑ Every major city in California
- ❑ Saw a Phillies Game in Pennsylvania

In most of these places I attended sporting events, NBA games, MLB games, college basketball games, or high school football and basketball games. Whenever a client asked if I wanted to go to a game, the answer was always *yes!*

I know I'm leaving dozens of other places out of this list. And it might sound like bragging but I'm not. Traveling is one of the perks of my profession and I make the most of it whenever I can.

When you love what you do, you never work another day in your life. I have been on "Holiday" for a quarter of a century. I will never retire. Why should I? I'm having too much fun "working" . . .

So do I HAVE to travel? Nope. I GET to travel!!!

## Your Ah-has? List Your Lights

*"Where in the world would I like to go?"*

_____

_____

_____

_____

_____

_____

_____

_____

_____

_____

_____

_____

_____

_____

_____

_____

_____

_____

_____

# MAN'S SEARCH FOR MEANING

*Everything can be taken from a man but one thing: the last of the human freedoms—to choose one's attitude in any given set of circumstances, to choose one's own way.*
—Victor Frankl, author

**In the early nineties I was lost.** By lost I don't mean I couldn't find my way home or LOST like the TV show where my plane crashed on a tropical island with black smoke monsters and polar bears. Lost as in, *Does my professional life have meaning and purpose?* I was the top salesman in my company, I had a loving wife, two beautiful young boys, a magnificent home with a sweeping view of Puget Sound and Mount Baker, and oh yes, an inground pool with a diving board. Yet I was at a crossroads. Is this all there is? By most standards I was living the American Dream. So why wasn't I content? Why did I feel sorry for myself?

I don't recall how I came to read Victor Frankl's classic book *Man's Search for Meaning,* but once I picked it up I couldn't put it down. It was the first time in my life I read a book in one sitting. You see, Mr. Frankl was a Jewish professor in Austria. He was captured by the S.S. and interned at Auschwitz. His wife, sister, mother, and father were killed by the Nazis. They took away everything, except for one thing: *his ability to choose his response to what was happening to him.* One night he made a decision. He would visualize a future whereby he was back in Austria speaking to a thousand students describing the death camp and how he survived it. He called it *logotherapy.* Inspired by his imagination, he set about serving others in the camp. He shared his food with other men. He encouraged them and told them there was hope. He was civil to his captors and did whatever he could to lift the spirits of others and himself.

My favorite life changing passages from Mr. Frankl:

*When we are no longer able to change a situation, we are challenged to change ourselves. What is to give light must endure burning.*

*Between stimulus and response there is a space. In that space is our power to choose our response. In our response lies our growth and our freedom.*

*Ever more people today have the means to live; but no meaning to live for.*

There it was. In the midst of Frankl's words was what I was searching for. *Meaning.* My life needed meaning. It wasn't enough to make a six-figure income. Meaning didn't come from material things or money.

Dr. Martin Seligman is a pioneer in the field of Psychology. In his book, *Learned Optimism,* he contends there are five factors for happiness:

1) Positive Emotions
2) Pleasure
3) Relationships
4) Engagement
5) Meaning

Of these five factors, he believes the last two, *Engagement* and *Meaning* are the most important. Becoming more engaged in what we do by finding ways to make our life more meaningful is the surest way to finding happiness. When our daily actions fulfill a bigger purpose, the most enduring and powerful happiness can happen. Perhaps *joy* is the better word. When we find meaning in our work, joy shows up and bolsters us with positive emotions, pleasure, and enhanced relationships.

Shortly after reading Mr. Frankl's book, my search for meaning became manifest. An old mentor of mine appeared in my life by way of a seminar. Over the next year, we reconnected several times. He eventually offered me a position in his business training and education company.

After much deliberation and prayer, I accepted. It was the most difficult decision I ever made. After almost four years with him, I went out on my own. Then I wrote my first book. Then another.

It's been over twenty-five years now. I write three pages every day. I speak to audiences around the world every week. I deliver keynotes, seminars, workshops, podcasts, coaching, and mentoring. My books and e-books are available on my website, Amazon, and Audible.com, and I have written hundreds of articles for magazines, LinkedIn, and Facebook. I have followed my bliss and today my work has true meaning.

No one has to tell me to get to work. I am self-employed. When I call in sick, I know I'm lying! I take off six weeks a year to spend time with my family. I used to save money and use people. Now I save people and use money. I have a wealth of friends and my life has balance. I work/play every day to make a difference in other people's lives.

I'll never know what it's like to be in a Nazi death camp or to lose my wife, sister, and parents to tyrants. But I do know this: I love what I do. It's a calling. I'll be doing it until my last breath. I am constantly amazed at how stupid I was two years ago. I keep searching for ways to improve the quality and quantity of my service to others. Money is the applause from my work, it's an effect. The cause is my service to others.

Would you like to earn more? Learn more! Serve more! Find meaning and purpose for and in your life. I had a poem on my office wall for years. It said, *Only one life, that soon is past. Only what's done with love, will last!*

Victor Frankl understood that when he said, *"I grasped the meaning of the greatest secret that human poetry and human thought and belief have to impart: The salvation of man is through love and in love."*

Today I am content. Today I am grateful. Today my life has meaning and purpose.

How about you? Why *not* you?

## Your Ah-has? List Your Lights

*"What gives my life meaning?"*

_____

_____

_____

_____

_____

_____

_____

_____

_____

_____

_____

_____

_____

_____

_____

_____

_____

_____

_____

*Window Eighteen*

# WHAT HAVE MENTORS TAUGHT ME?

*In learning, you will teach, and in teaching, you will learn.* —Phil Collins, musician

**Recently,** on a three-hour drive to our condo on Lake Chelan, I listened to *Meditations* by Marcus Aurelius on Audible.com. Though I have the book, listening impacts a different part of the brain. The wise old Roman begins by listing what he learned from various mentors. It was a laudable list of brilliant minds from the early Roman thinkers (think Maximus, Socrates, etc.). Marcus was a sponge.

It got me thinking about what I learned from various mentors over the years going all the way back to the

8th grade. Who were my mentors, and what have they taught me?

### Bob Stalder - my eighth-grade woodshop teacher

*When you start a project, see it through to the end. Finish what you start.*

*Give all your attention to the task at hand. Focused effort creates a solid end result.*

*If you love what you do, it's not work. It's play.* (I did thirty-one extra credit drawings for Mr. Stalder's mechanical drawing class and got an A+!)

### Bruce Evans - sophomore basketball coach

*Mark is hot! Get him the ball!* (If your player is hot, keep him in until he's not!)

*Score off a pass, not off a dribble.*

*What wins basketball games? It's simple, not easy: defense, free throws, and rebounds!*

## Susan Hall - my eleventh-grade German teacher

*You are better than this Mark!* (She had high expectations for all her kids, but me in particular!)

*Immerse yourself into the language. Watch German films, eat at German restaurants, associate with German-speaking people. Speak it as often as you can.* (My mother-in-law was German. Who knew?)

*Come speak to this group of kids at the high school. You have a great story of transformation to tell . . . "* (She pushed me into the speaking business without me even knowing it!)

## Bob Wilkes - journeyman pipefitter

*Be a sponge. Borrow boldly from the best.*

*Become a student of the craft. Observe, ask questions, and most importantly, learn from your mistakes.*

*You have a responsibility to the customer to fix it right the first time. Thank the customer for the privilege of serving them. They are the reason you have a job.*

**Les Dicks - national sales manager of the year, Xerox**

*If your boss says present two proposals a week, you do four! Sales is a numbers game!*

*The first six months, no one expects you to sell much. Go the extra mile.*

*Sales is simple. It's about activity and attitude. People buy from you for four reasons: trust, relationships, competence, and timing."*

**Bob Moawad - international speaker, coach, facilitator**

*Compare and compete with your own best self. Stop comparing yourself to others.*

*First we work on goals, then they work on us.*

*Affirm your goals and relax. Repetition is the mother of skill. Flip back on a previous WIN and remember it, re-feel the positive emotion, then fast forward to the new goal. Memory and Imagination are powerful twin pillars of goal achievement!*

*Let go of resentment, righteousness, and guilt. Life is too short to be chained to the past. It's over and done.*

## Charlie "Tremendous" Jones - bestselling author, publisher, international speaker

*You will be the same person in five years except for two things: the PEOPLE you meet and the BOOKS you read!*

*People who don't read have no advantage over people who don't know how to read. It's a kind of chosen illiteracy! The books you don't read won't help!*

*When you hug someone, who lets go first?*

## Zig Ziglar - international speaker, bestselling author

*Every year, get a check-up from the neck-up!*

*People don't care how much you know until they know how much you care!*

*It really is true, you can have everything you want in life, everything you want, if you just help enough other people get what they want FIRST!*

**Jim Rohn - speaker, author, business philosopher**

*Discipline is the bridge between goals and accomplishment.*

*You cannot change your destination overnight, but you can change your direction overnight!*

*Success is doing ordinary things extraordinarily well.*

**Earl Nightingale - audio learning pioneer, radio host, author**

*The one thing you cannot hide, expect by silence, is your vocabulary.*

*The Strangest Secret in the World? We become what we <u>think</u> about!*

*Exceptional people have adopted two unique philosophies. First, they are grateful. The second is they are expectant. Gratitude and optimism. Consider the opposites: sarcasm and pessimism. Which will you choose?*

Who were your mentors? What did you learn from them? A little personal reflection will uncover insight that you didn't know you adopted. You are smarter than you give yourself credit for. I'd love to hear your list.

I need to re-read *Meditations*. Marcus Aurelius knew a few things . . .

## Your Ah-has? List Your Lights

*"What have mentors taught me?"*

_____

_____

_____

_____

_____

_____

_____

_____

_____

_____

_____

_____

_____

_____

_____

_____

_____

_____

_____

_____

## *Window Nineteen*

# LIFE ISN'T FAIR?

*Life is a rotten lottery. I've had a pretty amazing life, a good life, and God knows I'm thankful, but I do believe that after age thirty, stop whining! Everybody's dealt a hand, and it's not fair what you get. But you've got to deal with it.* —John Waters, filmmaker, actor, writer

**Why do some people seem to drift through life** without any challenges or setbacks—their life is one unbroken boulevard of green lights—while others are hit with one crisis after another, like Job in the Old Testament. Life isn't fair? That's true. But in the end, it's not what happens but how we respond that counts!

*Knocked down seven times, stand up eight. Adversity doesn't make the man—it reveals him to himself."* —Phil Jackson, NBA Coach

The only person who likes change is a baby with a wet diaper! Nonetheless, change happens and it's usually best to embrace it and seize the opportunities it presents. Here's a piece I wrote about the stages of awareness, transformation, and CHANGE. I call it "Street Scholar."

*I walk down the street with shoes on my feet,*
*I step in a hole 'It's not my fault!' I shout*
*I wonder why I'm on this street,*
*I eventually pull myself out.*

*A week later on the same street,*
*in the hole I go again with both feet.*
*It's takes a while to get myself out,*
*But this time I do not shout.*

*Same street, I see the hole,*
*My eyes are wide open, not shut.*
*My denial is gone but it's taking its toll.*
*It's my own damn fault that I'm in a rut,*

*I walk down the same street,*
*I'm much smarter this time,*
*I walk around it with my two feet,*
*With a song in my heart and a catchy rhyme.*

*Today I have chosen a different street,*
*I guess that makes me a street scholar,*
*I'm proud of myself, ain't that neat?*
*Bursting with pride, I want to holler."*

Each of us must come to a place of expanded awareness based on experience and pain. We decide to change when we have had enough. Inspirational dissatisfaction. Sick and tired of being sick and tired. No one can do this for us. Pain is a great motivator. Physical pain, spiritual pain, mental pain, interpersonal pain, emotional pain, financial pain.

In my fourth book, *It's About Time,* I wrote about the Five Levels of Competence. Much of our unhappiness comes from a lack of awareness. We simply don't know. There are five levels or stages of competence.

## Stage One - Unconscious Incompetence

We don't know that we don't know. We are clue-less in Seattle (or wherever you live). In this first stage, we are blissfully unaware of our ignorance. Ignorance is not bliss. An absence of knowledge, attitude, skills, or habits is the worst kind of poverty. The first time I had my own camera was in London at age eleven. I used the whole roll of film—twenty photographs—to take pictures of animals at the London Zoo. My big sister tried to warn me. When I paid to have the pictures developed, they were a huge disappointment. She just laughed. That was Stage One, Unconscious Incompetence.

## Stage Two - Conscious Incompetence

We know we don't know. This knowledge is the beginning of change. Some intrepid and caring friend says to you, *You don't have a clue!* or *Why did you say that?* It's a wakeup call of sorts. There was a time in my life, in my late teens and early twenties, when it was more important for me to be right than to be happy. One fine day a friend called me on it. I woke up. Let me be clear; I didn't change right away, but I knew I soon had to. I simply didn't know how. It would have been nice to have a few pictures of people, especially of loved ones, in

London. Now I knew. A painful learning model is bad judgment, experience, and finally good judgment.

## Stage Three - Conscious Competence

We know we know. A measure of skill, focus, concentration, and teachability exists. We do some homework. We talk to others about how to improve. We ask questions. We take notes. We try new things. My second camera was more expensive and took better pictures. I became more selective about my choices and made certain the sun was behind me in shots I took. At night I made certain I was not too far away for the flash to work effectively. The quality of my pictures improved. I even received a few compliments. Mind you, I wasn't winning any awards, but I was making progress. They were pictures worth seeing.

## Stage Four - Unconscious Competence

We turn our behavior over to the subconscious. The work becomes easier, habitual, and less stressful. We operate on instinct and habit. I began carrying my camera with me and taking shots I knew would look good. I invested in a really nice camera. Just when I thought I was making progress, my wife showed me her Yashica 35mm camera and taught me how to use it. Wow, did the quality of the pictures improve! I considered entering some of my pictures in contests. I kept the best ones in a binder. Someone said to me, "You have a great eye." That was Stage Four.

**Stage Five - Unconscious Conscious Competence**

We finally arrive at a unique and fulfilling stage, mastery. We don't have to think about being good at something; we simply act. We are able to effectively teach what we know to others. Our knowledge is broad and extensive, our skills world-class, and our attitude positive, enthusiastic, empowering. Our habits are second nature. My pictures are ready for public consumption. Positive feedback is the norm. Time and tide have washed away all the bad judgment. What remains is worthy of note. Stage Five is a wonderful place to be. A picture is worth a thousand words! The picture I took of the Sydney Opera House is proof that I walk down different streets.

Life ISN'T fair. I think it's time to walk down another street.

How about you?

## Your Ah-has? List Your Lights

*"What one skill could I hone and improve?"*

_____

_____

_____

_____

_____

_____

_____

_____

_____

_____

_____

_____

_____

_____

_____

_____

_____

_____

_____

_____

_____

## Window Twenty

# OVER! NEXT?

*Life is made up of small pleasures. Happiness is made up of those tiny successes. The big ones come too infrequently. And if you don't collect all these tiny successes, the big ones don't really mean anything.* —Norman Lear, TV producer, writer, icon

**I was listening** to an interesting and thought-provoking podcast in the airport while waiting for a flight to Minnesota. Oprah was interviewing the television icon, Norman Lear. In his prime he was known as "The Prime-Time Provocateur." Are you old enough to remember the number-one shows he produced? They include *All in the Family; Maude; Good Times; The Jeffersons; Mary Hartman, Mary Hartman; One Day at a Time;* and *Sanford and Son.*

It's safe to say he was a genius in his field. At one poignant moment in the interview, he says, "It's vital to understand *'Over!'* and *'Next?'* when it comes to career choices."

Wow! That is so profound. The average guy you meet on the street never fully grasps the significance of those two words. Let's examine further.

**Over!**

When it's done, it's done. It's knowing when it's time to stop. It's Jerry Seinfeld going out on top, even when NBC offers him five million dollars an episode to continue. Seventy-five million people were watching his show when he walked away! It's Larry Bird retiring because the pain in his back was just too great. It's Gene Hackman retiring from Hollywood to write novels. Everything has a lifespan, an expiration date. Arnold shouldn't make another movie. His time as an action hero has passed. The moment you feel like you have to prove your worth to someone is the moment you absolutely need to walk away. Knowing when to walk away is *wisdom*. Being able to is *courage*. Walking away with grace, your held head high . . . well, that's *dignity*.

**Next?**

Move on. Let go. Shift gears. What are you looking forward to? Take a risk. Get out of your comfort zone. Jerry Seinfeld still does stand up. But when he got the idea for *Comedians in Cars Getting Coffee* he knew it was his NEXT? (He combined the three things he loves, comedians, cars, and coffee. Brilliant! He created a brand-new online genre!) I like to call it "My New Next!" It's the next chapter in your life. It's reinventing your career and life. It's NOT retirement. We need work to have meaning and purpose. Proverbs 29:18 says *"Where there is no vision, the people perish: but he that keepeth the law, happy is he."* We must have something to look forward to. It adds years to our life and life to our years. What is your New Next?

When I was in high school, my absolute favorite player was William Theodore "Bill" Walton III, UCLA's All-American center. After winning national championships in college, he led the 1977 Portland Trailblazers to an NBA championship. Perhaps the unluckiest guy in the league, he had more injuries than Imelda Marcos had shoes. Yet in 1986, playing for the Boston Celtics, he was Sixth Man of the Year and was the glue, the catalyst for yet another championship. Perhaps the most well-read ex-

NBA player, his New Next was becoming a color commentator first for the NBA, and now the Pac-12 announcer. He is arguably the most despised and loquacious announcer in sports. (When he is announcing I push mute and watch the game without his senseless and annoying ramblings!) But hey, you either love him or hate him, but he overcame a lifelong stutter to do something no one felt he could or would do. He has announced for thirty-one years. I admire him for that.

*It's time to say goodbye, but I think goodbyes are sad and I'd much rather say hello. Hello to a new adventure.*
—Ernie Harwell

*Every day is a new day, and you'll never be able to find happiness if you don't move on.* —Carrie Underwood

So just how do we embrace those two words, "Over!" and "Next!" in our lives?

1) Admit that whatever it is you are doing is done. It's over.
2) Ask yourself, "What is the next chapter in my life?" Think, ponder, ruminate, consider.
3) Capture as many ideas as you can in a journal.

4) Go for quantity not quality. Examine the choices later. Then pick one idea.
5) Run it by mentors who have done what you want to do and been where you want to go.
6) Follow your heart, not your head.
7) Take action. If it succeeds, celebrate. If it fails, do an autopsy.

Life is short. Well, maybe not for Norman Lear (he's ninety-six!) But for the rest of us, we must remember his advice: "OVER!" and "NEXT?"

I think I'll go on YouTube and watch an old episode of *All in the Family*. Rob Reiner was such a Meathead!

## Your Ah-has? List Your Lights

*"What is OVER? (What do I need to let go of?). What is my new NEXT?"*

_____

_____

_____

_____

_____

_____

_____

_____

_____

_____

_____

_____

_____

_____

_____

## *Window Twenty-One*

# PASSION + PREFERENCE + PREPARATION + PERSISTANCE = POWER

*Ambition is the path to success. Persistence is the vehicle you arrive in.* —Bill Bradley, senator and former NBA star

**Why do some people stay** in a job they hate for over thirty years? It's been said that "A rut is a grave with the ends kicked out!" Are you in a rut? I have an old friend from the neighborhood who is absolutely miserable. He has been at Boeing for thirty-five years and hates his life. He has a lot of toys. He pretends to be enjoying himself but we all know the truth. He has a serious drinking problem, his children don't talk to him, his wife has a restraining order against him, his friends avoid him. But hey, he works at Boeing.

What are you passionate about?

What are your preferences?

What kind of preparation do you engage in?

How persistent are you in going after your goals?

**Passion + Preference + Preparation + Persistence = Personal Power!**

When I was five years old, we lived on an air force base in Japan. I grew up listening to musicals like *The King and I* and *West Side Story*. One fine day, while the class was singing the national anthem, I broke out into a flawless rendition of "The Jet Song" from *West Side Story*.

I was sent home with a note pinned to my coat. It led to a parent-teacher conference to discuss Mark's behavior. In third grade I taught the class to sing pub songs I had learned in England over the summer.

In fourth grade, I made Mr. Hopkins laugh which led to an encouraging compliment from a man I admired:

*"You have a fine sense of humor."* It was the first time my public antics were praised. In seventh grade, Mrs. Dosser gave me an A for a story I wrote. I was over the moon with joy.

Mark, it turns out, likes to write and seems to be good at it. Never mind I flunked sophomore high school English! I discovered that writing has nothing to do with English!

Passion and preference trump what other people think, say, or do to you. If you believe in what you do, love what you do, follow your bliss, and are persistent (blisters), things have a way of turning out for the best.

Persistence, it seems, has been the one redeeming quality that has sustained me as a speaker and writer. *Kaizen* is a Japanese business philosophy of continuous improvement of working practices, personal efficiency, and persistence. Improve one percent a day for ninety days and you'll be twice as good at your work.

When my children were young, I said to them over and over, like a mantra, "In this family, we finish what we start!" If they heard it once, they heard it a hundred times. I only had a year of junior college, then I quit and joined the USAF. I didn't finish that either. My apprenticeship in Local 32, a four-year commitment, was the first thing I finished. That accomplishment set the table for my future success.

Maybe you've heard of Sisyphus? According to the annals of antiquity, he was doomed to punishment in the underworld. The penance for his trickery? King Sisyphus was made to roll a huge boulder endlessly up a steep hill only to have it fall back down before he reached the top. The maddening nature of the punishment was due to his hubristic belief that his cleverness had surpassed that of Zeus himself.

The key to long-term success, I believe, is to know when to cut your losses. My friend at Boeing never figured that out. He is still pushing his boulder up that hill. For me, my work is play, ten hours a day. I found my bliss and blisters.

How about you?

## Your Ah-has? List Your Lights

*"What am I passionate about?"*

_____

_____

_____

_____

_____

_____

_____

_____

_____

_____

_____

_____

_____

_____

_____

_____

_____

_____

_____

_____

_____

## *Window Twenty-Two*

# WHAT DO YOU REALLY WANT?

*I don't focus on what I'm up against. I focus on my goals and I try to ignore the rest.* —Venus Williams, tennis star

**The mind is powerful.** We can program it to achieve anything we want. I first discovered this when former state championship boy's basketball coach Bob Moawad came to our high school to speak at an assembly. Most of the kids couldn't care less what this man had to say. My situation was different. Just two years before I had been cut by my junior high school coach. Little did I know that was the day my life would change forever. It was in the wake of that bitter disappointment that I set my first real goal— a nascent vision. I really, *really* wanted to make the team the next year. So I sought advice from the best player I knew. His name was Kenny. He suggested two simple strategies:

1)   Shoot two hours a day, every day.
2)   Attend a basketball camp over the summer.

I did both, with passion and preference. Rain or shine, I shot two hours a day. I earned the money on my own to attend the camp. At that camp I gathered up valuable game experience and confidence. Moreover, I learned WHAT to practice during my daily two-hour sessions. The next season, my name was on the roster. You see, I had set a goal that really mattered to me. At fourteen years of age my life was about to change forever. My self-image was reset. I WAS good enough. Basketball gave my young life meaning and purpose, an outlet for all my youthful energy. It became part of my identity. I was bitten by the basketball bug.

First, we work on a goal. Then the goal works on us. As I navigated through this exciting new world, in addition to the sound advice I followed, I also committed to the following actions. Why? Because faith without works is dead.

1)  I read every book I could find on basketball.
2)  I devoured the sports pages and magazines, all things hoops.
3)  I found older boys to play against every day.
4)  I found all the open gyms and played four to five times a week.
5)  I watched every game I could on TV.
6)  I convinced my father to put up a court in the back-yard.
7)  I asked questions and found older boys to give me advice and encouragement.

Then along came a man who offered strategies on the mental side of the game. Coach Moawad was promoting a two-day *Mental Management* seminar. I convinced my mother to drive me to Seattle University on Super Bowl Weekend in 1971 and pay the forty-five dollars for the seminar, vowing I would pay her back. I learned:

1)  How to set exciting written goals on three-by-five cards.
2)  How to use my imagination to visualize those goals twice a day.

3) That anything I could imagine in my mind's eye with positive emotion was worth sixty times the actual experience!

4) WHAT and WHY were all I needed to get started. The HOW would come in time.

5) "Affirm the goal and relax." Repetition is the mother of skill.

6) Self-esteem and self-confidence go hand in hand. Success breeds success.

7) G.I.G.O. = Garbage In, Garbage Out. I learned how to manage my thoughts and input.

8) Words (positive or negative) trigger pictures and bring about emotion.

9) Attitude determines altitude.

10) Flip back on a WIN, hold the positive emotion, then imagine what you want to happen. Flick back, flip up. Rewind and fast forward.

*The new year stands before us, like a chapter in a book, waiting to be written. We can help write that story by setting goals.* —Melody Beattie

*Setting goals is the first step in turning the invisible into the visible.* —Tony Robbins

What is it you really, *really* want? Perhaps it's more money, or a beautiful home, a level of fitness, or improved relationships. Whatever it is, write it down. Make sure it's yours. Make sure it's what you really want. With the faith of a child, begin this process. Life is short. Go for it. What have you got to lose?

I wonder if that basketball camp is still there? I wonder what Kenny is up to now? I need to thank him.

## Your Ah-has? List Your Lights

*"What do I really want to achieve? WHY do I want it?"*

_____

_____

_____

_____

_____

_____

_____

_____

_____

_____

_____

_____

_____

_____

_____

_____

_____

_____

_____

## *Window Twenty-Three*
# WHY I WANDER

*You can never get a cup of tea large enough or a book long enough to suit me.* —C.S. Lewis

**I browse bookstores**—all kinds of bookstores—at least twice a month: Amazon, Barnes & Noble, Goodwill, independent bookstores, used bookstores, even an occasional garage sale (that's where I found an almost new, clearly unread copy of Dale Carnegie's classic, *How To Win Friends and Influence People* in 1982 for fifty cents!).

I like to wander. Why? Because I never know what I will stumble upon. I was having lunch with my speaker friend Kelly Schols in Mt. Vernon, Washington, a lovely town 36,000 people north of Seattle. Across the street from the pizzeria is an extraordinary used bookstore where I acquired a hardcover first edition of *Autobiography of Andrew Carnegie* for nine dollars! When the muse strikes, I wander. I invariably find a jewel, a gold nugget, a bargain.

I read fifty pages a day every day. That's anywhere from an hour to two hours depending upon what I'm reading. I borrowed this habit from Larry McMurtry, an American novelist who wrote the 1985 Pulitzer Prize-winning novel *Lonesome Dove*. His other books have been made into films such as *Terms of Endearment* and *The Last Picture Show*. He read fifty pages a day. If you want the results other people get, do what they do. Borrow boldly from the best.

It never fails, I get at least one great idea in the first twenty to thirty minutes of reading a book. Mind you, I read from many genres—biographies, memoirs, business, sales, spiritual, self-help, sports, humor, and books of quotes. I am partial to out-of-print books written before 1950.

Think about this: If you simply read for twenty minutes a day, or ten pages, that's seventy pages a week, 280 a month (two books), 3,640 pages a year (twenty books). That's a hundred books in five years! Can you see how the habit of reading good books can change your lifestyle and income?

In that twenty minutes of reading, if you only get one great idea, that is seven ideas a week, twenty-eight a month, 336 ideas a year! You only need one or two really great ideas to change your life, business, and income. I don't know about you, but I can't afford not to read for twenty minutes a day! They key is making reading a *habit*. First we form habits, then they form us. Consistency is the key.

*Clearly one must read every good book at least once every ten years.* —C.S. Lewis

At this point you might be saying, "Hey, I'm not much of a reader. I try to read at night in bed and fall asleep." I get it. If this is you, here are some ways around that:

1) Read first thing in the morning
2) Listen to Audible.com (books on audio) while driving
3) Listen to podcasts while driving
4) Have someone read to you while you drive
5) Buy condensed versions of books
6) Go to bookstores and listen to authors read from their books

I recently interviewed British author Roy Newey, a very successful businessman, on my podcast (subscribe at www.SparkingSuccess.net). His book *Ready, Set, Grow!* is available on his website. He left school at sixteen. He is dyslexic; he can't read! He found a way around that. He is a brilliant listener, a keen observer, he has a photographic auditory memory, he remembers everything anyone told him and he solicits feedback to get the information he needs. He told me a story:

*I was head of an economical revitalization committee in Liverpool. I was given a seven hundred-page report to read. I can't read. So I came up with a plan. In a very large meeting of very intelligent leaders who had all been given the report and had most definitely read it, I said, Let's go around the room. I'd like each of you to share the two most important things you learned from this report. As they shared, I listed them. Everyone was delighted because we pulled the salient points out of that seven hundred-page report and everyone was involved! I never read the report.*

Roy is the exception to the rule. He is a serious student, a wildly successful entrepreneur, and one of the finest story tellers I have ever met or interviewed.

I read two books a week. I don't tell you that to impress you. I flunked high school English and have one year of college. I tell you because now you know "Why I Wander." I need to keep a full funnel of books.

Remember this simple maxim: *"You will be the same person in five years except for two things: The people you meet and the books you read!"*

I think I'll stop by Barnes & Noble today. I have a gift card I need to use. I'll wonder as I wander . . .

## Your Ah-has? List Your Lights

*"How many pages will I commit to reading daily?"*

_____

_____

_____

_____

_____

_____

_____

_____

_____

_____

_____

_____

_____

_____

_____

_____

_____

_____

_____

## *Window Twenty-Four*

# THE TUGBOAT

*Prayer is when you talk to God. Meditation is when you're listening. Playing the piano allows you to do both at the same time.* —Kelsey Grammer, actor, director

**I live on the beach** in quant little Edmonds, Washington, a town so boring that when the tide goes out, it doesn't come back! Almost every day, I see something worth talking about. Whales, sea lions, eagles snatching a fish of the water.

This morning, in the midst of my daily "Hour of Power" (reading, praying/listening, planning) I watched a tiny tugboat push a gigantic old ferry boat that was out of commission and on its way to be repaired or, worse, the boneyard. Tugboats are the "AAA Tow Trucks" of the high seas. They show up when boats are stranded to save the day and get them to a safe harbor.

The first tugboat—the *Charlotte Dundas*—was built by William Symington in 1801. She had a steam engine and paddle wheels and was used on rivers in Scotland. Paddle tugs proliferated thereafter and were a common sight for a century. Compound steam engines and scotch boilers provided three hundred horse power. Steam tugs were used in every harbor in the world, towing and ship berthing. Modern tugboats have diesel engines and typically produce 700 to 3,400 horse power.

If you think about, when we pray, we are asking whatever higher power we believe in to give us a push, ever so slowly, to shore and safety, just like a tugboat. We all need a safe harbor. Moreover, we all need a tugboat from time to time. The vagaries of life guarantee that. No matter who you are or what your beliefs may be, one thing is certain: Your ship or ferry boat will need a push one day. If the only prayer you ever say in your entire life is "Thank you for the push," that will be enough.

H. Jackson Brown Jr. wrote *Life's Little Instruction Book* in the early nineties. It was a love letter to his son, who was going off to college. He wrote: *"Never forget the three powerful resources you always have available to you: love, prayer, and forgiveness."* And they are free . . .

I found a prayer this morning that I plan to say every day for the next thirty days, you know, as a test. It seems to fit me where I am, just like H. Jackson Brown Jr.'s book did for me in 1993. I hope you like it.

### *Release Me*

*God, keep me from the habit of thinking I must say something on every subject and on every occasion. Release me from wanting to control everybody's affairs. Keep my mind free from the recital of endless details—give me wings to get to the point. I ask for grace enough to listen to the tales of others' pains—Help me to endure them with patience, but seal my lips on my own aches and pains— they are increasing and my love for rehearsing them is becoming sweeter as the years go by.*

*Teach me the glorious lesson that occasionally it is possible that I may be mistaken. Keep me reasonably sweet. I do not want to be a saint—some of them are hard to live with—but a sour old person is one of the crowning works of the devil. Give me the ability to see good things in unexpected places, and talents in unexpected people—and give me the grace to tell them so.*

*Make me thoughtful, but not moody; helpful, but not bossy. With my vast store of wisdom, it seems a pity not to use it all, buy you know God, that it would be nice to have a few friends at the end.*

Jeff Crooks, an old friend from high school, was a tugboat captain for years. Maybe I'll give him a call. Riding a tugboat is on my bucket list. I need a little push. Don't we all?

## Your Ah-has? List Your Lights

*"In which area of life could I use a push?"*

_____

_____

_____

_____

_____

_____

_____

_____

_____

_____

_____

_____

_____

_____

_____

_____

_____

_____

_____

# *Window Twenty-Five*

# GUMPTION

*A winner is someone who recognizes his God-given talents, works his tail off to develop them into skills, and uses these skills to accomplish his goals.* —Larry Bird, NBA icon

**My brother-in-law Mike** and sister Sue told me recently that they came across an old letter our mum wrote to her mum—who lived in England—in 1976, explaining my plans to join the USAF had been delayed by six months. The delay was based on my desire to secure the job of HVAC technician as opposed to some random job they would select for me. So I waited. I had just finished my freshman year of college. I was eighteen years old.

To earn extra money so that I might finance a trip to Southern California, I started a window cleaning business. I was qualified, as I had been the sole window washer at 24108 107th Place West, Edmonds, Washington, my childhood home. *Find a need and fill it.* Most people hate washing windows. I liked it. There was a beginning, middle, and end—and the results were clear (pardon the pun). I would listen to the radio and whistle while I worked.

Back to the letter. Mum wrote, *"Mark has started a Window Washing Business and is very busy doing two houses a day. When things get slow, he puts up signs on telephone poles in affluent neighborhoods, knocks on doors and hands out business cards. He has GUMP-TION!"*

Webster's defines gumption as *"shrewd or spirited initiative and resourcefulness; enterprise, guts and imagination."*

What a lovely affirmation.

Do you have gumption? How does one get gumption? Is it nature or nurture?

I suspect I have always had it. As long as I can remember, I figured out what I wanted and learned how to ask for it. What follows is advice from a former window washer, submitted for your approval.

1)   Set a goal. What do you *really* want?

2)   Write down your WHYs—list the reasons you want it. Look at it several times a day and see it in your mind's eye.

3)   Be willing to get out of your comfort zone and try something new. If you fail, so what? Start again.

4)   Take action. Ready, Fire, Aim!

5)   Gather up the lessons learned and persist.

6)   Hang around other self-starters, preferably those who have done what you want to do and been where you want to go, and seek their counsel.

7)   Read everything you can find on the subject in your spare time, articles from trade journals and magazines, ezines, ebooks, and books.

If you are looking to hire someone with gumption, here are some clues:

1) Hire someone who has failed in business—give them a second chance.

2) Hire a man or woman who was all-state in high school sports—the work ethic and drive are already hardwired.

3) Look for kids who grew up on a farm. They have a great work ethic.

4) Find Eagle Scouts or Girl Scouts with tons of merit badges. I married a woman who had more than any other Girl Scout she ever met.

5) Find a candidate whose parents were or are CEOs or small business owners—the apple stays pretty close to the tree!

I'm re-reading *Moneyball* by Michael Lewis. Oakland A's GM Billy Beane is a man with GUMPTION. The man changed baseball. He was a pioneer, a risk-taker, he didn't care what people around him thought. He revolutionized the sport using previously unused or unknown metrics based on a simple principle: *"To win games with a smaller budget than any other team in baseball, you had to score more runs. To do that, you had to find players who could get on base. Walks were as important as hits."* In 2002, with a budget that was one-third that of the New York Yankees, he won twenty games in a row and made the playoffs. If you can't find a copy of the book, at the very least watch the movie with Brad Pitt as Billy. It will show you what gumption looks like in action—against all odds.

I miss me mum. I think I got my gumption from her. I think I'll make some tea and look at some old pictures. In 1976, I was skinny and had hair . . . and GUMPTION!

## Your Ah-has? List Your Lights

*"Do I have gumption?"*

_____

_____

_____

_____

_____

_____

_____

_____

_____

_____

_____

_____

_____

_____

_____

_____

_____

_____

_____

# *Window Twenty-Six*

# A LEGACY OF BOOKS

*Outside of a dog, a book is a man's best friend. Inside of a dog, it's too dark to read.* —Groucho Marx

**As long as I can remember, I have loved books.** It's with great affection I recall devouring the *We Were There* series at my elementary school library. I read every one. I was nine.

When our oldest son Colin was in second grade, we received some surprising news one fine November day— he was near the bottom of his class in reading level and aptitude. "What? I exclaimed. "That can't be. He loves books! I read to him every night." (It turned out, when he was supposed to be reading, he was joking around with his friends—I wonder who he got that from?) I resolved to change this.

I went to the school library and asked the librarian to help me. Librarians love to help with all things books. I asked her for five books at the second-grade level, five at the third-grade level, and five at the fourth-grade level ("chapter books!"). I signed for them and took them home like a prehistoric hunter dragging a deer carcass back to the family cave. I was on a mission, to feed him with the *want to* of reading books and inspire my son to read at a fourth-grade level.

When Colin came home that afternoon, I announced my grand plan: "Every one of these books represents ten dollars toward the purchase of a Nintendo! If you read all fifteen before Christmas, I'll drive you to the store and buy it for you" (All his friends had it and he was begging us to buy it for him for Jesus's Birthday).

He studied each book carefully, only looking at the top few—second-grade level books. "Okay," he said.

"Oh, one more thing—you must write a short paragraph or a long sentence on what you learned from the book. Deal?"

"Deal," he replied with all the enthusiasm of a long-shoreman. Nonetheless, he devoured all fifteen books in three days and off we went to the video game store.

Two days later he sauntered into my home office with six new chapter books that he had checked out from the library. "What's up?" I asked.

"I want a new video game!" Clever lad.

Andrew Carnegie, the man largely responsible for the public library system in the United States, wrote in his autobiography, *"So it seems I come by my scribbling propensities by inheritance—both sides, for Carnegies were also readers of books and thinkers. I only echoed what I heard at home."*

Abraham Lincoln was once quoted by a reporter, *"The things I want to know are in books. My best friend is the man who'll get me a book I [haven't] read."* Amen, Abe.

In hindsight, my wife and I did seven simple things to inspire our children to become lifelong readers of books:

1)   We kept books around the house and took books on all our family trips.

2)   We went to Barnes & Noble once a week as a family.

3)   We read to them every night (After age ten, and up until age fourteen, I read them classics like *The Old Man and Sea, Of Mice and Men,* and *Old Yeller*).

4)   I made certain when they came home from school, they found ME reading books.

5)   We used TV as a reward, not a right.

6)   Once they began asking me to rebound for them in basketball, I made another deal: *"If you read for an hour, I'll rebound for an hour . . ."*

7)   We rewarded reading behavior at every turn with effusive praise in front of their grandparents.

My son recently sent me a jpeg of his two girls, Penelope and Sawyer, reading books on their own—sitting on the couch at home (they are five years and eighteen months old, respectively). It made my heart soar. What a lovely legacy—*a legacy of books.*

Emilie Buchwald wrote, *"Children are made readers on the laps of their parents."* How true.

## Your Ah-has? List Your Lights

*"Do I read books to my children and grandchildren?"*

_____

_____

_____

_____

_____

_____

_____

_____

_____

_____

_____

_____

_____

_____

_____

_____

_____

_____

## *Window Twenty-Seven*

# WOULD YOU RATHER BE RIGHT OR HAPPY?

*A man wrapped up in himself makes a very small bundle.*
—Ben Franklin

**In my youth** I was concerned about being right. It was more important than almost anything else. One day, a mentor said to me, *"Would you rather be right or would you rather be happy?"* It was a rock in my shoe. That's what the right questions can do—they make us think hard about our philosophy, our attitudes, our beliefs, our habits.

Since that time, I've noticed a few other negative habits that are the kissing cousins of Must-Be-Right-At-

All-Costs—to me they are like fingernails on a chalk-board. In no particular order:

1) **The Sentence-Finisher** - These folks are the epitome of impatient and rude. They feel the need to jump in and try to speed up the conversation. More often than not, they are wrong because they weren't really listening in the first place.

2) **The One-Upper** - They usually are just waiting to talk, not really listening—waiting for a break so they can jump in with, *"That's nothing. One time at band camp I . . . "* To them, it's a competition not a conversation.

3) **The Corrector** - Usually very smart, often with multiple degrees but no social graces, insisting on telling you your facts are wrong—whether a baseball stat, song lyric, or the correct pronunciation of *Pecan*.

4) **The Prosecutor** - They may or may not be an attorney, but they act like one with everyone they meet by asking *leading questions* as a tool to bring up their agenda (I have an annoying brother-in-law who does

this to everyone in a social setting, so he can talk about *short snorting!* Don't ask!!).

5) **The Braggart** - No explanation needed.

All five share some common traits: A low self-esteem, a big ego, and a total lack of empathy.

In Ben Franklin's autobiography, he recalls getting feedback from a Quaker elder who confronted him about his confrontational attitude and overwhelming need to always be right: *"Young man, your opinions have become very expensive, few man can afford them."*

To Mr. Franklin's credit, he took the stinging rebuke with aplomb. From that day forward, instead of arguing his position, he began saying, *"I could be wrong, I often am . . ."* and *"You make a valid point, let's keep discussing it . . ."* What young Ben discovered was he dramatically decreased conflict and, more often than not, his views were received more readily and compromise replaced conflict. In other words, he decided he would rather be happy than right!

I have always admired successful men and women who were humble, like the head coach who holds the Super Bowl trophy and says, *"It was our coaching staff and players who deserve all the credit. This belongs to them."* To my way of thinking, humility and being teachable are one and the same thing. Humble people take feedback, avoid arguing, consider all the input, then shift gears and change.

Why do some people insist on being right over being happy? Pride, ego, fear, low self-esteem—it's a long list. Life is too short to argue, arm wrestle, and defend your position.

The next level of awareness on this topic is when someone calls you by another name (I get *Matt* instead of *Mark* because my last name is Matteson). I resist the urge to correct them. They eventually hear their mistake and apologize. I'm always happy I didn't correct them. I'd rather be happy than right.

Remember Ben Franklin's quote: *"In success be moderate. Humility makes great men twice honourable."*

## Your Ah-has? List Your Lights

*"Do I see a bit of myself in any of the five negative examples?"*

_____

_____

_____

_____

_____

_____

_____

_____

_____

_____

_____

_____

_____

_____

_____

_____

_____

_____

_____

_____

_____

_____

*Window Twenty-Eight*

# BREAKING BARRIERS

*It seems that most of our limitations are self-imposed.*
—Bob Moawad

**You might not remember a time** when the world believed no one could break the four-minute mile in track and field. *"It's impossible. No man can run that fast,"* the experts espoused. It seemed to be the truth. However, on the morning of May 6, 1954, a Thursday, a twenty-five-year-old London medical student worked his usual shift at St. Mary's Hospital and took an early afternoon train to Oxford. He had lunch with some old friends, then met a couple of his track teammates, Christopher Chataway and Chris Brasher. As members of an amateur all-star team, they were preparing to run against Oxford University.

About 1,200 people showed up at Oxford's unprepossessing Iffley Road Track to watch, and though the day was blustery and damp—inauspicious conditions for a record-setting effort—a record is what they saw. Paced by Chataway and Brasher and powered by an explosive kick, his signature move, this young man ran a mile in under four minutes—3:59.4, to be exact—becoming the first man ever to do so, breaking through a mystical barrier and creating a seminal moment in sports history.

His feat was trumpeted on front pages around the world. The *New York Times* declared that he had reached "one of man's hitherto unattainable goals." His name, like those of Babe Ruth, Bobby Jones, and Jesse Owens, became synonymous with singular athletic achievement. Then, astonishingly—at least from the vantage point of the 21st century—at the height of his athletic career, he retired from competitive running to concentrate on medicine.

He was born on March 23, 1929, in the London suburb of Harrow. His father, a civil servant, had been a runner of sorts: He won his school mile. He wrote in his memoir, "and promptly fainted afterwards—as so many runners did in those days." The young son ran, too, both for the thrill of it, he wrote, and out of fear, to steer clear of bullies and in response to air-raid sirens, which he heard as a boy in World War II during the Battle of Britain.

Professor William James of Harvard wrote, *"Compared to what we ought to be, we are only half awake. We are making use of only a small part of our physical and mental resources. Stating the thing broadly, the human individual thus lives far within his limits. He possesses power of various sorts which he habitually fails to use."*

Why is that?

For some of us, we feel we don't deserve good things in life and business. It's a self-worth issue. Many of those feelings come from childhood conditioning. A dog who has been hit over and over again flinches when his master raises a hand, even if it's to pet him.

For others, they listen to naysayers and critics. If we are told over and over again by ignorant teachers, coaches, parents, or relatives that we will never amount to anything, we begin to believe it. Repetition—Emotion—Time.

Still others surrender to defeat after one or two attempts. Quitting too soon is what the largest percentage of the population does without knowing that if they just kept going, things could change for the better. Worth—Belief—Surrender.

What if you *are* worth it?
What if you *believed* you could?
What if you *kept going*?

I have been sober for over forty-one years. Why? I just kept going, one day at a time. I have been a professional speaker for twenty-five years. Why? I just kept going, one day at a time. I have written six books and fifteen eBooks. Why? I just kept writing every day, one day at a time.

Imagine if you could achieve the things you really want in life and business?

It's simple, not easy. *"Figure out what you want in life and business—and learn to how to ask for it—and just keep going, no matter what. If you do, you just might break some barriers."*

Why not you?

Roger Bannister, who broke the four-minute barrier, died at age eighty-eight. His limitations held him back—until they didn't.

## Your Ah-has? List Your Lights

*"What if I just kept going?"*

_____

_____

_____

_____

_____

_____

_____

_____

_____

_____

_____

_____

_____

_____

_____

_____

_____

_____

_____

_____

## *Window Twenty-Nine*
# PIANO LESSONS

*Enjoy present pleasures in such a way as not to injure future ones.* —Seneca

**When our oldest son Colin was ten years old,** my wife insisted he take piano lessons—after all, *she* had to when she was his age. She might as well have said *"Every week, you are going to have a root canal. Isn't that a great idea?"* He had all the enthusiasm of a cat going for a walk. It was clear he didn't want anything to do with piano lessons. I made a note.

After a year, he had his first recital. He was terrified. His body language told the whole story. He kept looking at me as if to say, *"Help me Obi-Wan Kenobi, you're my only hope!"* It didn't go well. Oh, everyone clapped politely for the appropriate amount of time. Afterward, he pulled me aside and said, *"Dad, get me out of piano lessons and I will work twice as hard on basketball. Pleeeeeease!"*

You see, I was his AAU Basketball Coach. I put my arm around him and said, "Let me see what I can do, son."

"Thanks, Dad . . ." he sighed. I could tell he was grateful. I pled his case to the supreme court—they ruled in our favor.

True to his word, he worked hard every day on every aspect of his game. He led his team to the Final Four at State his junior and senior year and earned a basketball scholarship to play at University of Alaska Fairbanks.

*We move toward pleasure and away from pain.*

It's a law, like gravity. Fear of criticism drives most people's behavior. No one wants to look foolish.

We never asked Evan, our youngest son, to take piano lessons. Instead, we enrolled him in three sports, basketball, baseball, and hockey. One insane day, he had games in all three sports. We got up at 4:30 a.m. and didn't get home until well past nine o'clock. Exhausted, I said, "Ev, ya gotta pick two!" sounding like Moe from the Three Stooges. He chose to drop hockey. In hindsight, it was the smart move—you don't see too many six-foot-eleven hockey players.

Research tells us *Who we are at five years old is who we will be as an adult.* It follows then that our interests, attitudes, and affinities at that tender age stay with us. The secret is to surrender to our bliss and blisters. The Japanese call it *ikigai.* It's doing what we love and sticking with it for a lifetime.

Malcolm Gladwell's 10,000 hours (or ten years, whichever comes first) has almost become a cliche. That being said, why do we as parents or grandparents try to shove things down the throats of our children when it's clear what they really want, like, and adore? It's the doctor who insists his son go to medical school despite the fact his son wants to paint or dance ballet.

As I mentioned in an earlier chapter, when we lived in Japan, I was sent home from kindergarten at age five for singing "The Jet Song" from *West Side Story*. The problem was one of timing . . . the rest of the class was singing the national anthem! I was sent home with a lovely note that said, *"Mark has a lot of energy. We just need to find a way to channel it in a more constructive way. Can we discuss next week in person?"* It was clear I was simply paving the way to become a speaker. At an early age, I knew I needed a stage.

In Jay Leno's memoir *Leading with My Chin,* he tells the story of his second-grade teacher pulling him aside one day and laying down a challenge—if he would behave during class (in other words, be quiet and stop interrupting), she would give him five minutes at the end of class to riff and crack up the students. "Deal," said Leno. She understood.

What follows is a bit of wisdom born from painful experience:

1) Let your children try lots of different things for the first five to seven years of their lives

1) Make note of the things they have an affinity for (even if it's not what you want or like)
2) Encourage them to continue to pursue those activities
3) Praise progress, not perfection; sustained effort over results
4) Enroll them in classes, workshops, and on teams with like-minded children who love that activity
5) Take lots of pictures and post them
6) Predict long term success for them; be hearty in your approbation and lavish in your praise

Colin and Evan both went on to play basketball in high school, college, and professionally overseas. There is nary a piano in sight!

"I'm just sayin . . ."

## Your Ah-has? List Your Lights

*"What are my children's affinities?"*

## *Window Thirty*

# FIVE SIMPLE WAYS TO MAKE PEOPLE LIKE YOU

*Tower Records was a place to meet your friends, your co-workers or a place to meet new friends who shared a common love of music, literature and all things cultural.*
—Colin Hanks, actor, director

**Why do some people attract strangers** and others repel? What if there were five simple but proven ways to get people to like you instantly?

If you are brave enough to get out of your comfort zone and adopt these five simple strategies, people will want to spend more time with you but won't really know why. They'll just like how you make them feel—about you and about themselves. How do I know? I've tested them over the last thirty-five years. They work. Let's be clear: These are not clever, manipulative strategies—they are a way of being, a philosophy, habits to form—that few people understand or actually do. Moreover, they work very well from the stage, on Zoom, and one-to-one.

1) **Have a go-to story** - When you tell a story, pay attention to the response. If your audience laughs or cries, you have struck a chord. Tell it again as soon as possible—but not to the same audience if you can help it. As you re-tell it, tweak and adjust it—improve it using effective pauses. Go to work on your timing. If it's a funny story, give your audience a chance to laugh. Wait . . . Comedy is a dialogue—your part is the story—their part is the laughter. Let them laugh. Remember, deep practice.

2) **Act out the story** - When you tell a story, you are playing a part, like a role in a play. Use your voice to emphasize certain aspects. Don't be afraid to do impressions—they don't even need to be good. I use a British accent when telling a story about my English mother. Use your whole body—move around, wave your arms. Think of it

as "human cartooning." Raise your eyebrows, smile, laugh uproariously, and have fun telling it.

3) **Use self-effacing humor** - Make fun of YOU. It tells the audience you are not afraid to poke fun at yourself. When you do it, *they* don't get to—so beat them to the punch. It tells your audience you are comfortable in your own skin. It will endear you to them. Choose something about yourself you can make fun of. Even if it isn't entirely true, that's okay. Lift up your spouse—"I married up!" or "My children are so much smarter than I ever was at that age!" or "I know what you're thinking, I thought this guy would have more hair!"

4) **Tell stories that lift other people up** - "She is the cool breeze in a stuffy room!" or "That guy has forgotten more than I will ever know!" It doesn't cost you anything to give someone else the credit. Word will get back to them. Say nice things behind someone's back. Become a "good-finder." People don't care how much you know—until they know how much you care!

5) **Ask well thought-out questions when you are not on stage—and actively listen to the answers** - This is the time to be "other-centered." Avoid the temptation to talk about yourself. You had your turn. Give others some "stage time." Ask open-ended questions (Who, What, Where, When, How, and Why?) and just listen, nod, smile, and say, "That's so great—you must be proud!" Ask "How did you get started in your industry?" or "How did you two meet?" It's magic. It's like rain to dry flowers.

There you have it. Five great habits to adopt and practice. You will be amazed at the results. Simple, not easy. It means getting comfortable being uncomfortable. You will attract key people into your life—you will win new friends—and influence others—and your income and popularity will increase. I promise.

Will you attract or repel? It's your choice.

## Your Ah-has? List Your Lights

*"What if I choose one of five habits to adopt and monitor the results?"*

_____

_____

_____

_____

_____

_____

_____

_____

_____

_____

_____

_____

_____

_____

_____

_____

_____

_____

_____

_____

_____

## *Window Thirty-One*
# PAST, PRESENT, FUTURE

*If you think you can [do a thing] or think you can't [do a thing], you're right.* —Henry Ford

**Yesterday I went into Victory Studios** in downtown Seattle to record a thirty-minute keynote that will be delivered virtually next week. What a brave new world in which we live! I had a ball. I did it in one take. My client was delighted with the finished product. I prepared like crazy. Here is the process, submitted for your approval.

1)      I asked the client what his objectives were—exactly what he wanted to achieve in the time I had. For me, thirty minutes is harder than ninety

minutes for one simple reason: "What do I leave out?"

2)     I "mind-mapped" what I wanted to deliver, then listed the points in order, making certain the segues were smooth.

3)     I kept in mind that keynotes are more about entertainment than education—but I still needed to blend my client's objectives with some learning and powerful takeaways.

4)     I gathered up my best signature stories that are tailored to his industry (he is the largest contractor in Arizona!).

5)     I began by wearing my COVID mask and then taking it off, followed by some self-effacing humor that worked.

6)     I typed up my "set list" (the stories, exercises, quotes I would use in order of importance), putting "key words" to remind me what to say on the videographer's iPad that was positioned next to the camera. This allowed me to maintain my focus on the camera, instead of looking down at notes.

7)     I moved around during my presentation, acting out stories. We placed markers on the floor so I

would stay within the camera's lens and not wander out of the shot.

8)     The night before and the morning of, I affirmed my "speaking goals" aloud a dozen times and visualized getting it done in one take.

9)     I added some new material that was in alignment with the client's objectives—the themes were "Think Different" and "We Got This!"

10)    I decided to have fun.

After reviewing the video later that day, I was confident we had a home run, but it wasn't until my client sent me an email to say he was ecstatic that I knew all the preparation was worth it. He confirmed we would enjoy a long-term relationship and that I would be coming down to Arizona a lot over the next few years.

One of my messages was simple, yet profound. It fell into the category of both universal and personal advice. I said:

1)     *Let Go of the Past* (Mistakes and sins of omission and commission)

2)     *Cherish the Present* (All any of us really has is today)

3)     *Envision the Future* (What do you look forward to?)

Part of me believes that the name of the studio helped. VICTORY Studios! It was . . . a victory.

Chance favors the prepared. I use a formula for my preparation: 5-1. I spend five hours preparing for every one hour of presentation. To the tyro that may seem obsessive. If you want to deliver a world-class presentation, remember what Sir Anthony Hopkins once said in an interview about preparation to act:

*I read every script 250 times. When the lights come on and the camera rolls, I abandon the script and just act.*

I went over my set list today after reviewing the video. I covered ninety percent of what I had prepared and in one take, and I stopped at twenty-seven minutes and fifty seconds. I did two bonus outtakes.

Chance favors the prepared.

## Your Ah-has? List Your Lights

*"How well do I prepare for my presentations?"*

_____

_____

_____

_____

_____

_____

_____

_____

_____

_____

_____

_____

_____

_____

_____

_____

_____

_____

_____

_____

_____

_____

## Window Thirty-Two

# LET'S HAVE AN *ADVANCE*

*Without reflection, we go blindly on our way, creating more unintended consequences, and failing to achieve anything useful.* —Margaret J. Wheatley, writer, consultant

**Friday January 1, 2021, in Edmonds, Washington.** It's forty-six degrees Fahrenheit with gray skies and a forty percent chance of rain—and a ninety percent chance of reflection and journaling. The next three days set the table for the rest of the year. It's not a RETREAT . . . it's more like an ADVANCE! I do it every year. I am not making resolutions. I don't believe they work. I'm a Goal Guy!

It all started when I accepted a sales position in 1989. My boss asked me what I thought I could sell in the coming year. I boldly predicted 150% of sales plan. I had been a technician for the ten previous years, so his expectations of me were fairly low. By year's end I had hit my target, I was 150% of sales plan. He was ecstatic. I was jacked.

As I mentioned previously, over the holidays I went into the office to organize my desk and files. That's when I stumbled across an article in *Contracting Business* magazine about bestselling author Harvey Mackay. It changed my life. Among the many other inspiring things I learned about Harvey, I discovered he read five hours a day. That blew my mind. It was also a rock in my shoe. I began reading books for one hour a day, then two hours, then three. My life exploded into change. I've never looked back.

One very old book I found in a musty used bookstore (the title has long since faded from memory) asked some great questions that I have since asked myself over these many years . . . and now I share them with you.

1)   What did I learn this past year? (What were the most profound lessons?)

2)      What were the blessings from this past year? (What was most meaningful?)

3)      What do I want to achieve this year? Five goals? Focus on the WHAT and WHY. The HOW will come. (The key is balance: Spiritual goals? Financial goals? Wellness goals? Family goals? Interpersonal goals? Learning goals? What skills do I want to hone and improve?)

4)      What is my purpose? Why am I here? (What gives my life the most meaning?)

5)      How can I increase my service to others (Knowing that my rewards in life are directly related to the quality and quantity of my service to others)

I used to go to the ocean for three days by myself. Now I live on the beach so I simply turn off my phone, unplug my TV, make a big pot of coffee, grab a fresh blank journal, put on some Bose headphones, and play some pleasant music (I'm listening to "Traditional Japanese Music" with lots of flutes and running water, very soothing).

I go back over my journals for the past year (I usually fill up four to five a year) to assist me in answering the five questions. I wrote in my first book, *Freedom from*

*Fear—"The palest ink is better than the strongest memory!"*

Moreover, I choose a book that I think might just inspire me. The one I've chosen for this year was suggested by my old friend Mark Sangerman (In 1992, by his able example, he challenged me to begin reading the *New York Times* every day). The book is *Think Like a Monk: Train Your Mind for Peace and Purpose Every Day,* by Jay Shetty. Thanks, buddy.

I can attribute much of what I've accomplished the last thirty-one years to this simple commitment to reflection and imagining. I love my life. I love my work. I love my family. I love my friends. I love my clients. I love living in the greatest country in the world. The best of 2020 will be the worst of 2021 for me and mine. How do I know? Because I am going to answer the five questions above and get to work this year to achieve them.

The best is yet to come . . .

I have learned a few simple truths over the last sixty-three years that have changed my life. What follows are a few nuggets from my journals:

1)  *"I need to figure out what I want in life and learn how to ask for it."*

2)  *"I become what I think about."*

3)  *"The books I don't read won't help."*

4)  *"I keep a journal so I can get FROM the day, not just THROUGH it."*

5)  *"Life is short. I choose to seize the day."*

6)  *"Today is the tomorrow I worried about yesterday!"*

7)  *"I reap what I sow."*

8)  *"Everyone I meet is looking for three things: Appreciation, Respect and Understanding."*

9)  *"I never learn anything when I am talking. Today I seek to dominate the listening."*

10) *"My children and grandchildren don't listen to a word I say—but watch every move I make."*

11) *"Every person I meet is my superior in some way."*

12) *"I am constantly amazed at how stupid I was two years ago and the cycle keeps repeating . . ."*


Gotta go . . . I've got some questions to answer . . . so I can ADVANCE!


How about you?

## Your Ah-has? List Your Lights

*"When will I schedule time to reflect on lessons learned and imagine a better version of myself?"*

## *Window Thirty-Three*
# LISTEN *UP*

*I remind myself every morning: Nothing I say this day will teach me anything. So if I'm going to learn, I must do it by listening.* —Larry King

**Jerry Seinfeld** does a brilliant bit about UP and DOWN:

*"Wait up!" That's what kids say. They don't say "wait," they say "Wait up! Hey, wait uuuuup!" 'Cause when you're little, your life is up. The future is up. Everything you want is up. "Wait up! Hold up! Shut up! Mom, I'll clean up! Let me stay up!" Parents of course are just the opposite. Everything is down. "Just calm down. Slow down. Come down here. Sit down. Put that down."*

My parents' generation was fond of saying, "Children should be seen and not heard." That may just be the worst thing I ever heard growing up. I made it a point to encourage my boys to talk about their days, their feelings, their ideas, their thoughts, their points of view. As parents and grandparents, we all need to "Listen UP!"

You probably never heard of Dick Bass. He was the son of a Texas oil baron who was known for going on ambitious mountain climbing expeditions and talking about them—at length—to anyone within earshot, including a man sitting next to him on a cross-country flight. Bass went on and on about the treacherous peaks of McKinley and Everest and the time he almost died in the Himalayas and his plan to climb Everest again. After over three hours of non-stop talking—as they were about to land, he realized he had done all the talking—and had not properly introduced himself. "That's okay," the other man said, extending his hand. "I'm Neil Armstrong. Nice to meet you."

Dick Bass needed to Listen UP!

In the early stages of my professional selling career, a mentor helped me close a large sale (In point of fact—HE saved my bacon and stepped in when I was struggling to finalize the deal!) In the warm afterglow of closing a $250,000 deal, he turned to me as we walked to the car and asked, "Have you ever studied Carl Rogers and the skill of 'Active Listening,' young man?"

"No," I replied.

"That's obvious . . ." was all he said. I invested the next year studying the Art of Active Listening. It changed my life.

Gary Noesner was the top hostage negotiator for the FBI for over thirty years. He said, *"I think a good listener is someone who is open to hearing someone else's experiences and ideas and acknowledge their point of view."*

I have been teaching corporations to "actively listen" for over twenty-five years. I share a simple formula that works. Let me be clear, this is not a clever strategy or sleight of hand to manipulate other people. It's a philosophy, a way of being. Along with empathy and kindness, it's what I call being "OTHER-centered." Listening actively is one component of that philosophy.

**L.P.Q.P**. = **L**isten actively, **P**ause three to five seconds, **Q**uestion to clarify, **P**araphrase emotions and meaning for understanding.

**Listen actively** means you are totally focused on the other person. You ask open-ended questions—Who, What, Where, When, How, and Why? "How did you get started in your industry?" Lean forward, take notes, nod, stay focused on meaning, intention, and most importantly—emotions.

**Pause three to five seconds** . . . is hard to do. We don't like uncomfortable silences. I literally count to five silently in my head. Eighty percent of the time, before I get to five— the other person will start talking again—it was a comma, not a period—a semi-colon, not the end of the paragraph! Just be silent and wait.

**Question to clarify** means asking, "How do you mean?" or "Can you give me an example?" You think you understand their intention or feelings—but probably not. Clarifying questions ensures you understand completely. The person talking will tell a story or provide an example. It's so simple, but it's not easy.

**Paraphrase for understanding** sounds like, "If I'm hearing you right, you are frustrated about the way your boss treats you," or "You're sad your previous vendor didn't keep their word . . ." If true understanding exists, they will exclaim "EXACTLY!" or "YES!" (always in upper case!).

I encourage my clients to write a listening goal on a three-by-five card that simply says: *I dominate the listening in every conversation and people enjoy being around me.* I dare them to read the card four or five times a day for thirty days. That's how long it takes to form a positive new habit. What follows is a test—the homework: *"For the next week or two, see if you can get every person you meet to talk about themselves for fifteen to twenty minutes without them knowing they are doing all the talking. It's simple, not easy!"*

Once this skill becomes a part of your DNA, people you meet will want to spend more time with you but won't know why. They will just like the way you make them *feel*. They will tell you things they don't tell their banker, barber, or best friend. Oh yes, *"I never learn anything when I am talking . . ."*

My good friend Larry Zollinger, one of the finest and most successful sales professionals I know, likes to say, "Listen twice as much as you talk." He claims he learned that from me—he is being modest and kind. He was already a great listener when I met him in Austin, Texas fourteen years ago.

I don't want to be like Dick Bass. I want to be like Neil Armstrong. After all, he has been to the Moon and back! How about you?

Jerry Seinfeld had it right. Slow DOWN and Listen UP!

## Your Ah-has? List Your Lights

*"What if I dominated the listening?"*

 

_____

_____

_____

_____

_____

_____

_____

_____

_____

_____

_____

_____

_____

_____

_____

_____

_____

_____

_____

## *Window Thirty-Four*

# TO LOVE AND BE LOVED

*Let us always meet each other with a smile, for the smile is the beginning of love.* —Mother Teresa

**Becoming a grandfather changed me.** It was and is a seminal moment in my life, when I realized that life goes on, and will continue to go on, long after I am gone. It's the proverbial shade tree that I get to sit under. It can be described in one word, LOVE.

Is there anything more important than to love and be loved?

I had a poem in my office for years that said:

*Only one life, that soon is past;*
*Only what's done with love will last.*

The first time I held my second grandchild, Sawyer (the Princess Warrior), I wept. They were not tears of sadness or grief, no, they were tears of joy. To hold this little creature, to cradle her in my arms, to hold her head in the nape of my neck and feel her breath on my skin, was simply magical.

What is love? We have all heard Paul of Tarsus's epistle so many times at weddings it has almost become a cliché:

*Love is patient, love is kind. It does not envy, it does not boast, it is not proud. It does not dishonor others, it is not self-seeking, it is not easily angered, it keeps no record of wrongs. Love does not delight in evil but rejoices with the truth. It always protects, always trusts, always hopes, always perseveres. Love never fails. But where there are prophecies, they will cease; where there are tongues, they will be stilled; where there is knowledge, it will pass away.*

That is one tall order. It's so much easier to be impatient, unkind, envious, boastful, proud, self-seeking, angry, resentful, dishonest, and afraid.

What does love mean to me?

It means we keep our word to others we love, even when it's inconvenient.

It means we comfort those in pain, when we are in pain ourselves.

It means staying the course, hanging in there, never giving up on others.

It means looking for the good in others, even though it's hard sometimes.

It means selflessly doing something thoughtful when we don't feel like it.

It means forgiving others when they clearly don't deserve it.

It means praying for someone we don't like, even when we don't mean it.

It means showing up early and staying late for people we care about.

It means saying "I'm sorry" and meaning it, then changing future behavior.

It means seeing things from someone else's point of view. Empathy.

It means separating the negative behavior from the person.

It means giving the other person the benefit of the doubt.

Is there anything more important than to love and be loved? I don't think so.

I choose love. Life is short. Too short to not love others. John Lennon was right: *"All we need is love . . ."*

I can't wait to see my granddaughters again. I have a lot of love to give.

## Your Ah-has? List Your Lights

*"How can I become more loving?"*

## *Window Thirty-Five*
# NEGATIVE NICKNAMES

*I pay no attention whatever to anybody's praise or blame. I simply follow my own feelings.* —Wolfgang Amadeus Mozart

**From age twelve to thirteen-and-a-half** I grew nine inches in eighteen painful months. I was a gangly, clumsy kid. Who wouldn't be? My knees ached constantly and I knocked things over with great regularity. It became an issue in my family and, frankly, a punchline and a callback, mostly with raised eyebrows or disgusted looks and non-verbal cues of frustration from my elders.

In 1969, our family visited my maternal grandmother and her husband in England. My step-grandfather,

Opa, was an impatient old curmudgeon who couldn't tolerate my awkward behaviors and occasional mishaps (the spilled glass, tripping over footstools, etc.). He coined the term *muckle-hummocks*. Every time I would trip, he would say it out loud in a sarcastic Scottish brogue. It wasn't a compliment. It was a cutting comment from a man who was afraid. His low self-esteem, inferiority, and fear-based attitude demanded he put me down to lift himself up. No one ever said anything to him. He was a bully. Passive-aggressive behavior often goes unchallenged. Unfortunately, I didn't know I could stick up for myself. "Don't make waves," my mother would say.

I looked up the definition. *Muckle* means large. *Hummocks* is a hill or knoll. Opa was calling me a large (clumsy) hill. Wow! How sad. Years later, when I became a good college basketball player, my mother was astounded at my transformation. I recall hearing the word *ballet* in her description of my on-court performance. Opa was wrong on a number of levels.

I never forgot his cutting remarks. I vowed to never do that to my kids or anyone else's.

Children, employees, friends, clients, and audiences rise to the level of expectation. Words trigger pictures and bring about emotion, positive or negative. Those images and words become self-fulfilling prophecies. Great leaders understand this and apply it to great effect, in organizations, schools, sports teams, and churches. *"Treat me as I am, I remain. Treat me as I can be, I become."*

My youngest son Evan was described as "a late bloomer" in high school. Everyone agreed he had great potential. Teachers' and coaches' expectations can predict academic and athletic blooming. Armed with that information, I predicted Evan's success from the time he was twelve until he was twenty-two: *"Your future is so bright, it burns my eyes to look at it. You will go so much further than I ever did in school, sports, and business!"* I said that to him hundreds of times. I gave him the nickname *Beast* (as in "beast on the boards!"). Guess what? He became a beast! His senior year in college at Texas A&M International University he led his team to the conference championship and playoffs and was voted MVP of the conference, an All-American, and was drafted in the NBA's D-League.

The principle is called *The Pygmalion Effect* according to a study by psychologist Robert Rosenthal in 1968. See this six-minute video:

https://tinyurl.com/ns7ywn2r

There are four factors for creating the Pygmalion Effect:

**The Climate (Environment) Factor** – The Leaders are simply nicer to their students and employees in the things they say and in their nonverbal communication.

**The Input Factor** – The teachers, coaches, and managers teach more and better material to the students, players, and employees. They expect them to learn it.

**The Response Opportunity Factor** – Children, players, and employees do better when they get a chance to respond. They call on them more often asking for feedback and let them talk longer.

**The Feedback Factor** – The kids, players, and employees get praised for good answers and get clarity and paraphrased feedback for low-quality answers, like "Yes, good, and in addition . . ." There is a synergy and collaboration to every interaction that makes them feel important and needed.

Does this work with employees and adults? You bet it does.

Our job is not to stick our toes in the water, it's to make positive waves! Stick up for your kids, your players, your employees, and your friends. Don't let the Opas of the world determine your worth/self-image or that of your children or employees. What if they're wrong? (Bullies usually are!). Believe in others and say so. "Your future is so bright it burns my eyes to look at it!" Just ask Evan. He and his lovely wife Gen are expecting a baby boy any day. I just know they will never call him Muckle-hummocks— just Late Bloomer and Beast!

## Your Ah-has? List Your Lights

*"What positive nicknames can I create for others in my charge?"*

_____

_____

_____

_____

_____

_____

_____

_____

_____

_____

_____

_____

_____

_____

_____

_____

_____

_____

_____

_____

## *Window Thirty-Six*

# THE COMMON DENOMINATOR OF SUCCESS

*It's not enough to have lived. We should be determined to live for something.* —Winston S. Churchill

**What is your aim?** What is your purpose? What is your intention? Why do you do what you do?

It was the spring of 2003 in Sacramento, California. I arrived a little early to inspect the rooms and secure the lay of the land for my upcoming keynote. I was the closing speaker for the general session of the annual Radiant Panel Association meeting. As I perused the agenda I noticed Dan Holohan was the opening speaker. He was also doing a book signing at 2:00 p.m. I had some time. I wandered over and introduced myself. Dan smiled and said, "Have a seat. We can talk while I do some book signings. Do you have some of your books with you? We can sell your books, too, while we chat." I liked him immediately.

For the next ninety minutes we sold and signed books and talked about the business of speaking. Dan is one the best marketers I have ever met (and a fine speaker as well). He is the consummate student. He is constantly changing, evolving, growing. "How did you get started in this business?" I asked.

He said something that really made me think. "Nineteen years ago I told my wife, the lovely Marianne, if we can put four girls through college with this business (writing and speaking) that would be great." There it was. An emotional reason!

I have three boys. Three great reasons to succeed. I borrowed his idea. *"Put three boys through college! Earn enough money speaking and writing through 2012 to put my boys though college!"*

There was my emotional reason. My WHY.

When I first started in sales, I came across a document that changed the way I saw my work. It was profound, it was significant, and it was old.

It was written in the 1940s.

The author's name was Albert E.N. Gray. He was promoted to sales manager after a very successful career selling life insurance. Now he was charged with the task of inspiring others to succeed. He was looking for the common denominators of success. After much study, thought, discussion, and reflection, he put his thoughts down on paper. Here is what he wrote:

**The Common Denominator,** by Albert E.N. Gray

*Several years ago I was brought face to face with the very disturbing realization that I was trying to supervise and direct the efforts of a large number of men who were trying to achieve success, without knowing myself what the secret of success really was. And that, naturally, brought me face to face with the further realization that regardless of what other knowledge I might have brought to my job, I was definitely lacking in the most important knowledge of all.*

*Of course, like most of us, I had been brought up on the popular belief that the secret of success is hard work, but I had seen so many men work hard without succeeding and so many men succeed without working hard that I had become convinced that hard work was not the real secret even though in most cases it might be one of the requirements.*

*And so I set out on a voyage of discovery which carried me through biographies and autobiographies and all sorts of dissertations on success and the lives of successful men until I finally reached a point at which I realized that the secret I was trying to discover lay not only in what men did, but also in <u>what made them do it</u>.*

*I realized further that the secret for which I was searching must not only apply to every definition of success, but since it must apply to everyone to whom it was offered, it must also apply to everyone who had ever been successful. In short, I was looking for the common denominator of success. And because that is exactly what I was looking for, that is exactly what I found.*

*But this common denominator of success is so big, so powerful, and so vitally important to your future and mine that I'm not going to make a speech about it. I'm just going to "lay it on the line" in words of one syllable, so* *simple that everyone can understand them. The common denominator of success—the secret of success of every man who has ever been successful—lies in the fact that <u>he or she formed the habit of doing things that failures don't like to do.</u>*

There it is. I need to call Dan and thank him. My boys all have college degrees.

## Your Ah-has? List Your Lights

*"What are my emotional reasons to succeed?"*

_____

_____

_____

_____

_____

_____

_____

_____

_____

_____

_____

_____

_____

_____

_____

_____

_____

## *Window Thirty-Seven*

# IT'S ALL ABOUT THE BUN

*Quality is not an act, it is a habit.* —Aristotle

**The best hamburger I ever had was in Chicago** at a place downtown called Joe's Seafood" at 60 East Grand Avenue. I've been there three times. Amazing food and service! Ironic, isn't it? A great hamburger at a seafood place! (Strictly speaking, irony involves a reversal. A traffic cop who has thirteen unpaid traffic tickets is ironic because that is not expected; or rain falls on a sun festival, or a guy named Mr. Tallman is actually short). But I digress . . .

Yes, the meat on that burger was ground sirloin. The simplicity was just as important, as it only had ketchup and mustard on it, and of course the bun! It was a brioche bun and it was perfect. There are some things you simply don't skimp on. Here is my short list of *Wow Products and Services* that radiate quality.

1) Always buy the most expensive toilet you can afford. Unplugging a cheap toilet was for years the bane of my existence as a landlord.

2) Invest in the most expensive shoes you can afford and buy two pairs. Never wear the same pair of shoes two days in a row! Rockports for comfort, Gucci for Style.

3) In 1983 I bought a navy-blue blazer for three hundred dollars. I had it for years. That sport coat never goes out of style.

4) A Mercedes-Benz diesel. It will last for over 300,000 miles. I know.

5) The iPhone. I have had three since 2008. All other brands fall short.

6) Levi's 501 jeans. A classic and they last forever. The older the better.

7) The Broadmoor Hotel in Colorado Springs, Colorado. The finest property (four hundred acres), and the quality of food and service is in a class by itself.

8) Beatles music. Fifty Years later, the lyrics, musicianship, and harmonies are flawless.

9) James Bond movies (*Goldfinger* is still the gold standard, pardon the pun).

10) Briggs & Riley luggage. Lifetime guarantee.

11) Nordstrom service and quality.

12) FedEx Kinko's service and quality.

13) Starbucks coffee (I was hooked when they only had the first three stores in Seattle in 1982).

14) Bruce Springsteen concerts.

15) Key lime pie in Florida.

16) Books by Steven King or John Grisham.

17) Art by Picasso or Gaugin.

18) Any movie by J.J. Abrams, Steven Spielberg, or Martin Scorsese.

19) Anything by Jerry Seinfeld and Larry David.

20) A Montblanc pen.

Almost everything on the above list smacks of quality and serve as the gold standard, exemplars in their industry. Never the cheapest, but almost always the best. We tell our friends and rave about why we love it. We are rabid fans.

It's never just one thing that makes the perfect burger or concert. It's all the little things combined. Quality is never an accident. It's the byproduct of years of trial and error, of failing forward. It's the near cliche of ten years or 10,000 hours.

I wonder if Joe's delivers? I feel like the perfect burger. I should probably download Uber Eats and see! (Wait, #21 is Uber!) Pass the salt, would you please?

## Your Ah-has? List Your Lights

*"What do I need to do to improve my quest for quality in my products or services?"*

_____

_____

_____

_____

_____

_____

_____

_____

_____

_____

_____

_____

_____

_____

_____

_____

_____

_____

_____

## *Window Thirty-Eight*
# PLUCK A THISTLE AND PLANT A ROSE

*The greatest legacy one can pass on to one's children and grandchildren is not money or other material things accumulated in one's life, but rather a legacy of character and faith.* —Billy Graham

**A client recently asked me** how I wanted to be remembered after I'm gone. Pausing for effect, I smiled and said, "I want people to say that I plucked a thistle and planted a rose where I thought it would grow." It's a quote from Abraham Lincoln. He should know. He experienced more adversity in twenty years than a dozen men do in a lifetime. He lost three of his four children. He was married to a woman who was described by others as a "wildcat" and "she-devil" and a "shrew;" she was arguably the meanest, most self-centered woman ever to live in the White House. As a young man, Lincoln lost his mother and the only woman he ever truly loved, Ann Rutledge. He grew up poor. He suffered from deep depression most of his life, and he was assassinated in 1865 at the age of fifty-six. So why is he considered the greatest president this country has ever seen? Persistence. Resolve. His ability to bounce back from setbacks and adversity.

Here is the famous list of Lincoln's failures. Don't think you have any chance of being successful? Based on his past record of failures, Abraham Lincoln had no right to think he could win the presidency of the United States. But that didn't keep him from trying. Consider this: Abraham Lincoln

- failed in business at age twenty-one.
- was defeated in a legislative race at age twenty-two.
- failed again in business at age twenty-four.
- overcame the death of his sweetheart at age twenty-six.
- had a nervous breakdown at age twenty-seven.
- lost a congressional race at age thirty-four.
- lost a congressional race at age thirty-six.

- lost a senatorial race at age forty-five.
- failed in an effort to become vice president at age forty-seven.
- lost a senatorial race at age forty-seven.
- **was elected PRESIDENT of the United States at age fifty-two!**

Positive opposites. Thistles to roses.

What follows are twelve positive opposites. Abe understood the human condition. He made others feel important. What if you focused each month on living Honest Abe's positive habits? You can't enjoy the rose without the thorns.

1)   Complain? Appreciate!
2)   Swearing? Clean language!
3)   Lying? Honesty!
4)   Tear others down? Build others up!
5)   Ignore people? Greet others with enthusiasm and use their names!
6)   Gossip? Praise!
7)   Blame others? Accept one hundred percent responsibility!
8)   Talk about yourself? Ask about others!

9)  Be sarcastic? Be sincere and laugh at yourself!
10) Talk too much? Listen actively!
11) Avoid eye contact? Make eye contact!
12) Sour-faced? Smile!

When you adopt these positive opposites, and make them a habitual part of who and how you are, you will attract more friends, influence others in positive ways, and enjoy long-term and healthy relationships. Moreover, you will pass these traits to your children and grandchildren.

What if you said the following on a regular basis?

*"Hello, Bob! Man, you look great! You've lost weight! What's your secret?*

*How is your family?"* (as you lean forward, hanging on their every word as you make eye contact).

After hearing their story, smiling, you continue, *"Good for you! You deserve it! I am so proud of your commitment and progress! We should get together more often. Here's my card. With your kind permission, I will stay in touch."*

How do you suppose people will respond?

*Good habits are hard to form, but easy to live with.*

These twelve habits will change your life in ways that will astound you. I am still working on making them a consistent way of being.

*Four score and seven years ago our fathers brought forth on this continent, a new nation, conceived in Liberty, and dedicated to the proposition that all men are created equal.* —Abraham Lincoln, November 19, 1863

Look over there! A thistle. Now where can I find some roses?

## Your Ah-has? List Your Lights

*"How good am I at bouncing back from adversity?"*

_____

_____

_____

_____

_____

_____

_____

_____

_____

_____

_____

_____

_____

_____

_____

_____

_____

_____

_____

_____

## *Window Thirty-Nine*

# IT'S ONLY A DIET COKE

*No act of kindness, no matter how small, is ever wasted.*
—Aesop

**Over twelve years ago** I gave up eating rubbish—donuts, cookies, brownies, candy, rubbish. Once in a blue moon I'll have a celebratory donut. I had a particularly good business week. And what do you know? There just happened to be a Top Pot Donuts (rated one the "Top 50 Places to Eat" in Seattle Magazine by the readers' poll!) close by, so I drove the quarter mile to get me some bad carbs, you know, that tasty deep-fried flour/sugar combo and a cup of joe. I was sitting in my car enjoying this tasty treat when I noticed a man about my age leave his car— that was lined up with others, like a procession of caterpillars, to catch the Kingston ferry—and enter Top Pot. Less than a minute later he came out empty-handed with a puzzled look on his face. He was looking my direction, so I rolled down my window and asked, "Can I help you find something?"

"Oh, I was looking to buy a Diet Coke but they don't sell them at the donut shop." Shaking my head, I replied, "Yeah, that's a tough one. I'm not sure you are going to find that around here, not close by anyway."

"Thanks," he said with his head down, and he returned to his car. As I pondered his situation it occurred to me, *I have some time. I have some money. Why don't I find that nice guy a Diet Coke?* I walked over to the fish and chip place and found a Diet Pepsi. It cost me $2.79.

Starting at the back of the line of caterpillars, I walked slowly, peering into each car, scaring half the people waiting for the boat. I finally found him and motioned for him to roll down the window. I smiled and said, "They didn't have Diet Coke, all I could find on such short notice was this Diet Pepsi" as I handed it to him through the window. His grin started slowly, eventually reaching just below his ears. For some reason, I handed him my business card and said, "Make it a great day . . . unless you have other plans."

"Thank you," he replied.

As I walked away, I felt like a million bucks! You see, my actions were in alignment with my new philosophy, *Work Smart, Be Kind, Help Others.* I've learned I can be happy if I get a gift from someone; but I can be just as happy, if not more, if I give someone a gift. It turns out there's no limit on how happy I can be. I just need to be kind and giving.

Two days later I received an email from the man in the car.

*Mark—you don't know how much your random act of kindness meant to me. For you to not just ignore me searching for a simple thing like a Diet Coke, but to take action and seek me out. Wow. I will pay this forward!*

*You caught me on an awful day after a marital disagreement with my wife and after experiencing "your position has been eliminated" news a few weeks ago. Your random act made a difference in my life yesterday—thank you.*

*I wish you much joy and success, Mark. Best to you and your family.*
*T. David Pyron*

Now this would be a good story if I left it there. But as Paul Harvey used to say, "Now, the rest of the story . . ."

The next week I was in Gaithersburg, Maryland speaking on *Customer Service Excellence* to a large and successful HVAC Service Contractor. I told that story. I asked the audience, "What kind of Diet Cokes can you surprise your clients with as you go about your day?"

After the seminar, a gentleman by the name of Keith was walking through the warehouse having just lit a fine cigar. It smelled good. I asked himn "Where might I find a good cigar store close by?"

He smiled and said, "Well, it's a ways from here." Pausing for effect, he continued, "Never mind, here you go!" and proceeded to hand me two Padrón cigars (A single Padrón usually runs around twelve dollars).

"Oh," I said. "I wasn't looking for a free cigar . . ."

Keith smiled again and replied, "Mark, it's just a Diet Coke!"

What can you do to make someone's day? What can you do to surprise people with unexpected and extra-mile gestures? Why not try a Diet Coke and a smile? You just never know what someone else is going through.

What do you know? It's another blue moon . . .

## Your Ah-has? List Your Lights

*"What acts of kindness can I bring to every interaction with others?"*

_____

_____

_____

_____

_____

_____

_____

_____

_____

_____

_____

_____

_____

_____

_____

_____

_____

_____

_____

## Window Forty

# TURN STRANGERS INTO FRIENDS

*A tree is known by its fruit; a man by his deeds. A good deed is never lost; he who sows courtesy reaps friendship, and he who plants kindness gathers love.* —St. Basil

**My Mother used to say,** "Mark never met a stranger." That used to make me smile. When I was five years old we lived in Yokohama, Japan. My favorite film was *The King and I*. I was enamored of Yul Brynner's portrayal of the King of Siam. There is even an old black-and-white picture of me with my pajama top open, right hand up in the air, imitating "The King" (evidently saying, *"Etcetera, etcetera, etcetera"*). In fact, the movie soundtrack offers a master class in how to turn strangers into friends: "Getting to Know You," performed brilliantly by Deborah Kerr. I have the lyrics memorized. I'm sure you've heard it. If not, look it up and give it a listen.

What follows are seven simple strategies for turning strangers into friends. They are timeless and reflect the human condition, at once both personal and universal.

1)  **Become genuinely interested in other people**. My high school German teacher Susan Hall taught me, *"Everyone has a story. Your job is to find out what that story is."* It turns out you can make more friends in five minutes being genuinely interested in other people than you can in five years of trying to get them interested in you. Do you remember **C.I.A.** = **C**ompliment them; **I**ntroduce yourself; **A**sk an open-ended question—like, "So how did you and your husband meet?" and then be sincerely interested in the answer—other people will open up and engage you in conversation.

2)  **Smile.** Did you know it takes forty-seven facial muscles to frown, but thirteen to smile? Evidently, most people don't mind the extra work! My old friend and Little League teammate Matt Saban always has a thousand-watt smile in this seventy-five-

watt world. His smile is sincere, continuous, and contagious. He genuinely loves people and is always glad to see you. Everyone loves Matt. Why not smile more? Take a look around, pay attention to how we try to make babies smile. Play peek-a-boo with every nine-month-old baby you meet and see how it makes you feel. You will make everyone else around you smile. It's universal.

3) **Remember other people's names.** The sweetest sound in every language is the sound of our name crossing the lips of others. The cigarette king of North Carolina donated forty million dollars in the 1920s to little Trinity College to convince them to change their name to Duke University (The stretch between Duke and North Carolina Universities is called "Tobacco Row" for a reason!). It's the greatest compliment when someone important or famous remembers your name. My friend Alex Carney once shared a simple way to find out someone's name you have forgotten. He smiles, reaches out his hand, and says: "We have met before, Alex Carney." They always shake his hand and tell him their name. Simple. Smart.

4)   **Dominate the listening!** That sounds like an oxy-moron, you know, like "back up forward" or "jumbo shrimp." I have earned more business the last forty years by simply asking open-ended questions (WHO, WHAT, WHEN, WHERE, HOW, and WHY) and sitting back to listen. People tell me things they don't tell their barber, banker, or best friend! We have two ears, two eyes, and one mouth. God is a genius. Why don't we listen more? Ego, pride, vanity, fear. I play a game on airplanes: *Can I get my seatmate to talk for thirty minutes without them knowing they are doing all the talking?* I win every time!

5)   **Talk in terms of other peoples' interests.** When my wife listens to someone she remembers every-thing. One day, I heard her ask a woman at church, "How is your daughter's leg?" Evidently, some months back, this lady's daughter had broken her leg. The woman was touched she remembered. When you listen, pay attention to the things the other person is concerned about, passionate about, and cares about. What is their hot button? Watch their face light up and the volume of their voice

increase. What exactly is most important to them? Remember it. Bring it up later.

6) **Make the other person feel important.** Pay attention to the other person's body language, pay attention to their clothes. I like baseball caps as a way to discover their passions. Whenever I see a Boston Red Sox or Oakland Raiders or Lakers cap, I comment or praise the success of that organization. Their face lights up and they talk about it with great joy. The secret is to be sincerely interested and say, "How did you come to be a fan of that team?" Then sit back and listen. It's magic (Pardon the pun!).

7) **Master the art of improv.** There is big difference between "YES and . . ." and "NO but . . ." YES and" is being other-centered and keeps the spotlight on others. It attracts others to us. "NO But" is a competition that pushes people away. "YES And" means you have developed the habit of observing, acknowledging, and heightening. It's what improv pioneer Del Close taught at Second City in Chicago. Simply say what you see or hear. "YES and" attracts abundance, joy, and faith. "NO but" creates lack, scarcity, and fear.

I just downloaded *The King and I* soundtrack. Man, that Deborah Kerr has a set of pipes. When I listen to that song I'm five years old again in Japan imitating Yul Brynner . . . *"Etcetera, etcetera, etcetera."*

## Your Ah-has? List Your Lights

*"What will I do to honor others and make them feel important?"*

_____

_____

_____

_____

_____

_____

_____

_____

_____

_____

_____

_____

_____

_____

_____

_____

_____

_____

_____

_____

## *Window Forty-One*
# OCCAM'S RAZOR

*Great leaders are almost always great simplifiers who can cut through argument, debate and doubt, to offer a solution everybody can understand.* —Colin Powell

**Unless you are student of history,** philosophy, or theology, you've probably never heard of Friar William of Ockham. He was born in 1285 and died in 1347. He was a Philosopher and Theologian. Educated at Oxford, he posited *"Any given set of explanations for an event occurring, the simplest one is most likely the correct one. It's a kind of 'shaving away' of unnecessary assumptions when distinguishing between two competing theories."* The concept is often used by detectives or doctors for effective diagnosis.

In other words: *"The simplest solution is almost always the correct one."*

If you walked into the doctor's office with some pain in your stomach and he took one look at you and said, "Let's get you some penicillin" you would flee! In sales and as in medicine, we must diagnose before we can prescribe.

To uncover and discover simple solutions to client's challenges, we must do three things well:

1) Ask well-planned and prioritized open-ended questions." Who? What? Where? When? How? and Why? to diagnose the situation.

2) Actively listen to understand the cause of the pain and the value of the solution. Listen, pause, question, paraphrase.

3) Offer a choice of yesses with two or three options.

I recently worked for the second time with a large tractor dealer in Omak, Washington. The question came up, "How do we sell value, not price?" This is where Occam's Razor comes in handy. Qualifying the prospect is the most important aspect of the sales process, but first we must follow a simple formula for discovery and diagnosis. This assumes, of course, that you are dealing with the "economic buyer" (that is, the person who can write a check and has fiduciary responsibility for the project). Here are the questions I've used for years to effectively diagnose, submitted for your approval:

1) Ask "How much time do we have today?"

2) Ask "How did you get started in this industry?"

3) Ask "What is the number-one issue that has you up at night?"

4) Ask (once you feel you understand) "What will it mean to YOU to overcome this challenge?"

5) Ask "What will it mean to your TEAM to achieve it?"

6) Ask "How will we know when we have achieved it?"

7) Ask "If we tripped over those results, what would they look like?"

8) Ask "What else do you think I should know?"

9) Ask "How are decisions made in this organization/family?"

10) Ask "If we could accomplish this, would that be something you would want?"

11) Ask "What kind of budget do you have?"

12) Ask "Why ME?"
13) Ask "Why NOW?"
14) Ask "What is the next step for us?"
15) Then say, "Okay, IF I can put some ideas together for our next meeting with some choices you might appreciate—can we discuss the value of those ideas in our next meeting? Is that fair enough?"

Notice I only asked one "closed-ended question." These are questions that begin with a verb: IF or DO or IS or ARE. They CLOSE the conversation. When you take this approach, you are tailoring the solution to the client's objectives. Like a great doctor, you are solving the problem with simple solutions. You are no longer competing, you are creating!

William of Ockham was right. "The simplest solution is almost always the correct one."

Albert Einstein once said, *"If I had an hour to solve a problem, I'd spend fifty-five minutes thinking about the problem and five minutes thinking about the solution."* That is how we sell value, not price!

I don't suppose you have any penicillin on you?

## Your Ah-has? List Your Lights

*"What questions do I ask others to assist them in solving their challenges?"*

_____

_____

_____

_____

_____

_____

_____

_____

_____

_____

_____

_____

_____

_____

_____

_____

_____

_____

## Window Forty-Two

# WE REAP WHAT WE SOW

*How people treat you is their karma; how you react is yours.* —Wayne Dyer

**Some things simply are.** There are laws that operate in life whether we are aware of them or not. Universal laws. Gravity is one. If you step off a twenty-five-story building you will always go down, never up. You will fall thirty-two feet per second until you are introduced to another law, *deceleration trauma.*

We reap what we sow. Cause and effect. Karma. We get back what we send out, positive or negative. If you plant corn, you will get corn. If you plant nightshade (a deadly poison), you get nightshade. The soil is neutral.

It doesn't care what you plant. Corn and nightshade will grow in equal abundance. Life and business are like that soil.

As children, we all heard the story of the *Goose That Laid the Golden Egg.*

> *A golden egg, one every day,*
> *That simpleton's goose used to lay.*
> *So he killed the poor thing,*
> *Swifter fortune to bring,*
> *And dined off his fortune, that day.*

The moral? "Greed overreaches itself."

A proverb is, by definition, *a short pithy saying in general use, stating a general truth or piece of advice.* Some of them are not quite clear at first glance—like *No good deed goes unpunished.* I never quite understood that one. So I looked it up. *"The phrase 'No good deed goes unpunished' is a sardonic commentary on the frequency with which acts of kindness backfire on those who offer them. In other words, those who help others are doomed to suffer as a result of their being helpful."* Thankfully, this is the exception most of the time, not the rule.

I gather from that maxim that some people will show their true colors in challenging or stressful times. *Adversity does not make the man, it reveals him to himself (and others).*

What I have come to understand—after being on the receiving end of betrayal from a troubled relative—is that there will come a time in every person's life when someone you have been kind and generous to for years does something unconscionable and you are left with the aftershock of selfish or immoral behavior. After the dust settles, what each of us is left with is a choice: resent or forgive.

I recently went through such a spiritual journey. I was forced through a narrow tunnel of grief and experienced grief's five stages: shock, denial, anger, bargaining, acceptance. After much reflection, prayer, and thoughtful consideration I determined that the results were not up to me. I recalled an old proverb from the Bible. What does *Vengeance is mine says the Lord* mean? It means God will vindicate the righteous and punish the wicked. He judges with perfect justice and perfect mercy. It's not up to me. We reap what we sow. I wouldn't want to be around when the Karma lands on my relative's head.

I'm working hard today on forgiving my enemies. It's a short list. Life is too short to let someone else rent space in my brain. I choose to replace malice with kindness, enmity with peace, resentment with forgiveness and prayer. Don't get me wrong, I won't forget, but I will let go, pray for those people, and move on. In the end, we really do reap what we sow.

I'm not going to step off any twenty-five-story buildings. I know what will happen. I'll be patient and wait for the elevator. Or, as the women in Texas say, "Bless his heart . . ."

## Your Ah-has? List Your Lights

*"What am I reaping?"*

_____

_____

_____

_____

_____

_____

_____

_____

_____

_____

_____

_____

_____

_____

_____

_____

_____

_____

_____

## *Window Forty-Three*

# TO BE TOTALLY WITHOUT STRESS IS TO BE DEAD

*It's not stress that kills us, it is our reaction to it.*
—Hans Selye

**McCarran Airport is a great place** to study the human condition. A few years ago, I had been working in "Lost Wages, Nevada" for three days. I checked out of my hotel early, took a cab to the airport hoping to get on standby as there were three flights leaving earlier. The answer was a hard *no* on three successive flights. After waiting six hours I ended up on my original flight. To make the most of the time, I purchased *Life of Pi* and sat back to read a good novel. My concentration was occasionally interrupted by groups of people arriving. They were laughing, walking, and loudly talking with purpose and excitement. They were on their way to winning big at the slots, black-jack, and roulette. They were delirious with anticipation about the shows, the glitz, the glamour that only Vegas can provide. They were experiencing "stress" in a positive way.

Hans Selye coined the term *stress* when referring to human life. In physics, *stress* is used to refer to the interaction between a force and the resistance to counter that force, and it was Selye who first incorporated this term into the medical lexicon to describe the *"nonspecific response of the body to any demand."* He began referring to the causes of stress as *stressors*, and he later advocated for dividing stress into the positive *eustress*, and negative *distress*. He was a nominee for the 1949 Nobel Prize, won many accolades, and published his best-known book, *The Stress of Life*, in 1956.

Back to my Vegas experience. The people I observed coming IN were experiencing eustress (a kind of positive anticipation, like young children the day before Christmas). The people going OUT were experiencing distress. It was obvious in their body language, their dejected and sober visages, their haggard and hungover demeanors.

Wayne Dyer, my late mentor, said it best: *"The truth is that there is no actual stress or anxiety in the world; it's your thoughts that create these false beliefs. You can't package stress, touch it, or see it. There are only people engaged in stressful thinking."*

So just what can we do to increase our eustress and decrease our distress?

Daniel Amen, M.D., in his marvelous book *Change Your Brain, Change Your Body,* offers this advice:

- **Pray and meditate daily.** Invest fifteen to twenty minutes a day in silence. Find a place to sit quietly, turn off your phone, say a little prayer, close your eyes and wait.
- **Take a yoga class.** It promotes calm and self-awareness. It reduces anxiety and depression, lowers blood pressure, and boosts your quality of life.
- **Delegate.** Focus most of your time on the "Best and Highest Use of Your Time" (in other words, do what you are good at and like most). Find other

people to handle what you don't like to do and are not good at doing. Stop trying to do it all yourself. Delegate.

- **Practice gratitude.** Every week, make a list in your journal of five to ten things for which you are grateful. Choose to be "Grateful, not hateful!" By focusing on what's great about your life and business, it breeds what Martin Seligman calls *learned optimism* which is linked directly to an increased sense of joy, happiness, longevity, and life satisfaction.

- **Get seven to eight hours of sleep.** Adequate sleep enhances your ability to fight stress. We need the time to rejuvenate and repair. Drink more water.

- **Walk it off.** Get to the beach or into the woods. A twenty-to-thirty-minute walk can change your mood. I walk through airports every week. I always take the stairs, I walk briskly to every flight.

- **Listen to soothing music.** Classical or ambient sounds work best. I am fond of Mozart and Bach. I listen to soothing music when I write and read. It actually enhances memory and fosters creativity. I am doing it now as I write this.

Hans Selye said it best: *"Adopting the right attitude can convert a negative stress into a positive one. The healthiest of all human emotions is gratitude. Stress is not necessarily something bad—it all depends on how you take it. The stress of exhilarating, creative, successful work is beneficial, while that of failure, humiliation or infection is detrimental. If you want to live a long life, focus on making contributions to others. To be totally without stress is to be dead.*

Maybe I'll take another trip to Vegas to see Louie Anderson. He always makes me laugh. Now that's the good kind of stress.

## Your Ah-has? List Your Lights

*"What am I looking forward to?" (eustress)*

_____

_____

_____

_____

_____

_____

_____

_____

_____

_____

_____

_____

_____

_____

_____

_____

_____

_____

_____

_____

_____

## *Window Forty-Four*

# DO YOU BELIEVE IN MAGIC?

*The world is full of magic things, patiently waiting for our senses to grow sharper.* —W.B. Yeats

**When I was ten years old,** my older brother brought home an album by the Lovin' Spoonful. When he put it on the turntable, the first song that came on was *"Do You Believe in Magic?"* John Sebastian's soulful voice filled the room. The rhythm guitar got my foot tapping. The harmonies rising to a crescendo made my heart soar. (To listen, visit https://youtu.be/JnbfuAcCqpY).

I was hooked. I believed.

In 1979, a sophomore point guard from Michigan State led his team to the NCAA men's basketball championship. I had never seen anyone quite like him. He *was* magic. You have probably heard of Ervin "Magic" Johnson. He's a legendary Hall of Fame NBA player. He was famous for winning championships at every level of his career, but his real gift was his unselfish play that made everyone better. In LA, he created *Showtime* and played point guard at six-foot-nine and 265 pounds. His no-look passes changed the game. He is now a very successful businessman in Los Angeles.

I had the privilege of meeting Magic Johnson in Las Vegas recently. We spoke for all of ten minutes in the VIP room. Later that morning, he closed the event with a fascinating one-hour keynote. He has a simple gift. He makes the people he meets feel important. As I studied him, it occurred to me: He is authentic, sincere, and honestly loves people. It's not an act. He has been doing it since junior high school. It doesn't hurt that he is rich and famous. But it begs the question—Is his extraordinary success in sports and business because of who he is and how he treats the people he meets? That is certainly a factor.

I noticed that he does seven simple things with everyone he meets:

1) He SMILES. He has a thousand-watt smile. It's inside, out. It's the joy of living. He is genuinely glad to meet you. Remember, it takes forty-seven muscles to frown, but only thirteen to smile (Some people don't mind the extra work). Magic Johnson gets it. His contagious smile puts you at ease.

2) He asks your NAME. He remembers your name. He uses it in conversation more than once. For each of us, it is the sweetest sound in the world. He gets it. He makes you feel important (even more so from someone of his stature in sports and business; he co-owns the LA Dodgers).

3) He ASKS you about something he knows is important to you. In my case, he asked about my sons. He went on to say, "Please say hi to them for me!" So just how did he know I had sons who played basketball? Magic.

4) He COMPLIMENTS you. We discussed working out. He makes the conversation about you. He never comes across as insincere.

5) He is POLITE. He says "Please" and "Thank You" every time. He is gracious and kind.

6) He LISTENS. His habit of actively listening to what you say is endearing. It's a dialogue. He is other-Centered.

7) He CARES. He communicates that caring with his body language, eye contact, and demeanor. He has real empathy for others. He always takes the time to take a picture with you or sign an autograph. He never comes across as "put-out."

Is he rich and famous because he is kind; or is he kind because he is rich and famous? I believe it's the former.

After reading a couple of books about him, two things stand out throughout his amazing career: *Work hard* and *be kind*. Be kind and work hard.

When we met, I told him a story about *him* . . .

*In his second year with the Lakers, Magic and Kareem Abdul-Jabbar were just finishing up a pre-game shoot-around in the Forum. A man and his nine-year-old son timidly approached Kareem and asked the seven-foot-two Hall of Fame center for a picture. Kareem said 'No' and walked off. Magic noticed the hurt in the young boy's eyes. He approached the man and said, 'I'm not in the Hall of Fame yet. Would you like to take a picture with me?' The little boy beamed. Magic smiled for camera. Twenty-two years later, Magic was pitching a business idea in a board room to the CEO of a major corporation. The man interrupted him and said, 'We met before, a long, long time ago. You probably don't remember, but Kareem blew us off, but you were very kind. You took a picture with my son and I. He's an attorney now. That picture of the three of us hangs on the wall of his office. The answer to your question about the deal is, YES!' Magic walked out of the meeting with a new multi-million-dollar client in his portfolio.*

After watching Earvin Johnson in Las Vegas, I've concluded he really is "Magic." It's not an illusion. It's real. He possesses teachable interpersonal skills anyone can adopt. Why not you?

Do you believe in magic? Be careful. There is a no-look pass coming your way!

Now where is my iPhone? I just know I downloaded that Lovin' Spoonful hit. That song still holds up, all these years later! I believe . . .

## Your Ah-has? List Your Lights

*"What habit can I borrow from Magic?"*

_____

_____

_____

_____

_____

_____

_____

_____

_____

_____

_____

_____

_____

_____

_____

_____

_____

_____

_____

_____

_____

## *Window Forty-Five*

# MAGIC MENTAL MANAGEMENT METHODS

**I have been studying *mental management* since 1981.** Forty Years of conversations, books, seminars, workshops, videos, audio programs, and hundreds of pages of journaling. What follows are Mark's Magic Mental Management Methods. Simple, not easy. I'm still working on them. What we are talking about is a kind of *emotional intelligence* (E.I.). Most people are smarter than they give themselves credit for. It's not more E.I. we need, but less. Less of these five bad habits. Less is more. First we form habits, then they form us.

1) **Rule 62 - Stop taking yourself so seriously!** I spoke to a large group a few years ago. There were over five hundred people in attendance. After my keynote, as I was

signing books, a gentleman said to me, "I really like your 'Self-Defecating' Humor!" I told him that was a crappy thing to say. He smiled—once he understood his faux pas.

Whenever I find myself taking life's challenges way too seriously, I remind myself to ask a few questions:

> *How important is this really?*
> *Will this really matter in ten years?*
> *What CAN I do?*
> *What is OUT OF MY CONTROL?*

George Carlin said, *"Don't sweat the small stuff—and don't pet the sweaty stuff."*

Why does Rule 62 work so well?

a) Most people don't do it. It's rare, unique.
b) It's a fun way to look at life.
c) I go from my head to your heart with humor.
d) It's authentic, real, genuine.
e) It builds bridges instead of barriers.
f) The more important your station in life, the more vital it is to remember and follow the rule of 62.
g) It will separate you from the herd.

I'm always amazed at how stupid I was two years ago and the cycle keeps repeating.

I end most conversations with "Make it great day, unless you have other plans!" Some people do . . .

2) **Worry is a misuse of the imagination** - A mentor of mine once told me, *"Worry is negative goal setting—it's a misuse of the imagination."* Why do most people worry? To reduce uncertainty. Worry gives us the illusion of certainty. Stop trying to change what hasn't happened yet. *Today is the tomorrow you worried about yesterday!* Worry is a kissing cousin of fear. F.E.A.R. = False Evidence Appearing Real. It's countless hypothetical scenarios played out in our minds over and over again—why? Somewhere in our journey we picked up this negative habit from a relative or a coach or a teacher and made it our own. Let me be clear, if you have blood coming out of your nose or a giant lump on your neck, go see a doctor right away. But worrying that you MIGHT die tomorrow or lose your job next week doesn't add value to your organization or your contribution to the business *today*. Focus on actions you can take today. Call the doctor and make an appointment. Work smarter, worry less.

3) **Endlessly criticizing others** - When you say to someone, "You're stupid . . ." it means you are really saying,
"I'm smarter . . ." Making sarcastic and hurtful comments
about someone else in public (or behind their back) is a
kind of moral superiority. It feels good in the short term
but acts like a cancer to the critic in the long term. Unless
you are being paid to write about movies or plays by a
news organization, ask yourself *"Why am I bashing this
person or place or thing?"* Any fool can criticize and
most fools do. I'm still working on this one . . .

Teddy Roosevelt said it best:

*It is not the critic who counts; not the man who points out
how the strong man stumbles, or where the doer of deeds
could have done them better. The credit belongs to the
man who is actually in the arena, whose face is marred
by dust and sweat and blood; who strives valiantly; who
errs, who comes short again and again, because there is
no effort without error and shortcoming; but who does
actually strive to do the deeds; who knows great enthusi-
asms, the great devotions; who spends himself in a worthy
cause; who at the best knows in the end the triumph of
high achievement, and who at the worst, if he fails, at
least fails while daring greatly, so that his place shall*

*never be with those cold and timid souls who neither know victory nor defeat."*

4) **Ruminating on the past** - Let go of the past. It's over and done. We must learn from the mistakes so we can make new ones. Stop mulling over past mistakes of omission and commission. Ed Pepple, one of the best basketball coaches I ever met, used to yell to his players: "NEXT Play!" Great advice.

Pastor Chuck Swindoll said it better than anyone:

*[Attitude] is more important than the past, than education, than money, than circumstances, than failure, than successes, than what other people think or say or do. It is more important than appearance, giftedness or skill . . . I am convinced that life is 10% what happens to me and 90% how I react to it. And so it is with you . . . we are in charge of our Attitudes.*

5) **Change our expectations** - For some people, unmet expectations are premeditated resentments. In our minds, we build up what *should* happen. What if it doesn't? *Should* is a slippery slope. So are *ought* and *must*. Let go. *It is what it is.* They are who they are. We can't control

other people. We can only change ourselves. Detach with love and move on.

I met Dr. Paul O. in 1986. He talked about expectations and serenity. He wrote about it too. Here is what he had to say:

*Acceptance is the answer to all my problems today. When I am disturbed, it is because I find some person, place, thing or situation—some facet of my life unacceptable to me, and I can find no serenity until I accept that person, place, thing or situation as being exactly the way it is supposed to be at this moment.*

*Perhaps the best thing of all for me is to remember that my serenity is inversely proportional to my expectations. The higher my expectations of other people are, the lower is my serenity. I can watch my serenity level rise when I discard my expectations. I have to discard my 'rights,' as well as my expectations, by asking myself, "How important is it, really? How important is it compared to my serenity, my emotional sobriety?"*

*I must keep my magic magnifying mind <u>on</u> my acceptance and off my expectations, for my serenity is directly* *proportional to my level of acceptance. When I remember this, I can see that I've never had it so good.*

*—The Big Book of AA*

There is nothing noble about self-centered righteousness.

There you have it. Five simple rules.

I turned them into affirmations as a way to review and adopt them into my life. I put them on a three-by-five card and plan on reading five times a day for thirty days. The best is yet to come.

1)    *I poke fun at myself before anyone else gets to.*
2)    *I focus on what I CAN do and let the rest go.*
3)    *I avoid criticizing others—I'm a good-finder.*
4)    *I let go of the past—acceptance is the answer for me.*
5)    *I lower my expectations of others so I can increase my serenity.*

As Rod Serling used to say, "Submitted for your approval . . ."

P.S. You probably never heard of John Burroughs (born April 3, 1837—died March 29, 1921). He was an American essayist and naturalist who lived and wrote after the manner of Henry David Thoreau, studying and celebrating nature. My favorite quotes from this brilliant man include:

*Leap, and the net will appear. A man can fail many times, but he isn't a failure until he begins to blame somebody else. How beautifully leaves grow old. How full of light and color are their last days. The lure of the distant and the difficult is deceptive. The great opportunity is where you are. A somebody was once a nobody who wanted to and <u>did!</u> The smallest deed is better than the greatest intention.*

Amen, John.

## Your Ah-has? List Your Lights

*"What can I let go of?"*

## Window Forty-Six

# THE PRIZE IN THE BOX

*Strive not to be a success, but rather to be of value.*
—Albert Einstein

**A German immigrant came to Chicago in 1872** to help clean up after the famous Chicago fire. He also worked selling popcorn from a cart. Together with his brother, he experimented and came up with a delightful popcorn candy, which the brothers decided to mass market. *Cracker Jack* was first mass-produced and sold at the Chicago World's Fair of 1893, the same fair that introduced the Ferris wheel, Aunt Jemima pancakes, and the ice cream cone were also introduced at this event. The treat was a mixture of popcorn, molasses, and peanuts. Its first name was Candied Popcorn and Peanuts.

Legend has it that the name Cracker Jack came from a customer who, upon trying the treat, exclaimed, "That's really a cracker, Jack!" The name stuck. However, *crackerjack* was also a slang expression that meant "something pleasing or excellent." This is more likely to have been the origin of the name. The Cracker Jack name was registered in 1896.

Cracker Jack's mascots, Sailor Jack and his dog, Bingo, were introduced in 1916 and registered as a trademark in 1919. Sailor Jack was modeled after the grandson of the founder. By 1896, the company devised a way to keep the popcorn kernels separate. The mixture had been difficult to handle, as it tended to stick together. The wax-sealed, moisture-proof box was introduced in 1899. Immortalized in 1908 in the lyrics of the baseball song "Take Me Out to the Ball Game," Beginning in 1912, Cracker Jack added surprises in each package. This tradition continued until Frito-Lay stopped the practice in 2016.

I never really cared for the Cracker Jack. It would stick to my teeth and, well, the *taste*. But man, did I love the prize at the bottom! I never knew exactly what I was going to get. McDonald's took a lesson from the makers when they created the Happy Meal. The kids don't care much for the food, it's the toy that counts! Every kid I ever met ripped open the box of Cracker Jack from the bottom to find out what prize was contained therein. After the joy of the prize wore off, then he or she ate the Cracker Jack.

What is it about the anticipation and excitement of the unknown? What could it be this time? I hope it's a unique toy that I can brag about! What if it's one of those cool press-on tattoos? For kids. it's all about "I have it and you don't!"

Our German immigrant friend understood *lagniappe,* a word derived from the South American Spanish phrase *la yapa* or *ñapa* (referring to a free extra item, usually a very cheap one). The term has been traced back to the Quechua word *yapay* (to increase; to add). In Andean markets it is still customary to ask for a *yapa* (a little extra) when making a purchase. The seller usually responds by throwing in a little extra. Although this is an old custom, it is still widely practiced in Louisiana. Street vendors, especially vegetable vendors, are expected to throw in a few green chili peppers or a small bunch of cilantro with a purchase.

What is the prize in the box that makes your product or service unique?

During the COVID pandemic, as I discuss options with clients regarding a keynote speech or seminar, I add a bonus, some webinars on sales or customer service to sweeten the pot. I might even toss in books for everyone in attendance. Lagniappe!

Do you offer that little something extra that your customers don't originally expect, but eventually come to love about you and your company? What if you sent a handwritten note or called after a repair or a project to see how happy they are? No one does that!

*"People don't care how much you know, until they know how much you care!"* —Zig Ziglar

It's been said that sales is an act of pure creativity and caring. The word for sales in some languages translates to the word service. How creative are you in demonstrating your caring to your prospects and clients?

My mother was the queen of the handwritten note and the thoughtful letter. Every night, before reading a book, she sat down at her writing desk and dashed off a well-worded thank-you note or two for a kindness expressed. I borrowed that habit from her. I need to do much more of that. There is something magical about a handwritten note with blue ink and paper. In this lazy, fast-paced, digital, tweeting world in which we find ourselves, a well-crafted, other-centered, handwritten note is priceless. Spoken words, regardless of how kind or caring, are "frost on a windshield." They are gone in a few minutes. A handwritten postcard, thank-you note, or letter goes a long way in building the relationship. Why? Because it's rare, uncommon, unique.

*"Too often we underestimate the power of a touch, a smile, a kind written word, a listening ear, an honest compliment, or the smallest act of caring, all of which have the potential to turn a life around."* —Leo Buscaglia

Joe Girard is in the *Guinness Book of Records* for selling the most cars in one year, 1,280. In his book *How to Sell Anything to Anybody,* he says, "I write postcards every day to my clients that simply say, 'I like you!'" He goes on to say, "Everyone knows 250 people. That is how many, on average, come to your wedding and funeral. What if you wrote five postcards a day to your top 250 existing clients? That means by the end of two months, every important client has heard from you, by the end of the year, six times. Six thoughtful gestures from you. Who do you think they are going to call when they need something?"

The power of a postcard. I considered why this was such a powerful proposition. Here are my top twelve reasons to try this:

1. It's so simple.
2. It takes five minutes.
3. It's so cost-effective, Twenty-five cents at Walgreens for the postcard and thirty-three cents for the stamp. That's fify-eight cents!
4. No one does it!
5. It doesn't get caught in a spam filter.
6. It says "I care about you!"
7. It positions you in top-of-mind awareness (My friend Adams Hudson calls it TOMA). It's "Remember me!" or Marketing 101.
8. It's creative, unique. (I buy mine on the road: Pismo Beach, New Orleans, Vegas, Chicago, Seattle, etc.).
9. It's fun. Some of the postcards are hilarious. Make people smile.

10. It's good business. It costs a dollar to keep a client, seven dollars to earn a new one!

11. Your clients will reach out to you and new business will happen (referrals, projects, products, and service requests).

12. Like a daily workout, it's good for me. It forces me to think of others. Once I get in the groove, I really enjoy it. It's an exercise in gratitude.

What if I don't have 250 clients? That's okay. To whom do I send them? Simple: customers, prospects, good friends, vendors, and relatives. All that matters is the discipline, the reps. Good things will start happening within ninety days.

What do you say six times a year? How about borrowing from other people who do this, like:

*"Thank you for your friendship, trust, or business"* (Mark Matteson)

*"You are tremendous, I thank God every time I think about you."* (Charlie "Tremendous" Jones)

*"I like you."* (Joe Girard)

*"To your massive success!"* (Kevin Knebl)

*"God gave me a gift of 84,600 seconds a day. I wanted to take one of those to say I am grateful for our friendship."*

*"Happy Birthday! (Okay so it's a little late, or early, does that really matter?)"*

My mother had about fifty really close friends because of her thank-you-note habit. By her able example I believe the seed of this idea was planted. Thanks, Mum.

President George H.W. Bush wrote five thank you notes a day beginning early in his political career. He claims it put him in the White House. By the way, so did Presidents Carter, Reagan, and Clinton. I can hear my male readers objecting. Hey, Ernest Hemingway, a man's man if there ever was one, was an avid writer of hand-written notes.

Why not send postcards to your top 250 for the next ninety days, just as a test. Even if your business doesn't double, your joy will. You never know, it might be the only card they ever get.

What if you got your team together and asked them on a regular basis, "What can we do to add a thirteenth donut in the box?" How can we improve our level of customer service and value both internally and externally?

A German immigrant, Frederick William "Fritz" Rueckheim, changed the way we looked at snacks back in 1893. Come on, sing it with me, you know you want to: *"Candy-coated popcorn, peanuts, and a prize, that's what you get in Cracker Jack!"*

## Your Ah-has? List Your Lights

*"How can I add value to my customers' expectations?"*

_____

_____

_____

_____

_____

_____

_____

_____

_____

_____

_____

_____

_____

_____

_____

_____

_____

## *Window Forty-Seven*

# AS YOU WISH AND WANT

*Figure out what you want in life—and learn how to ask for it!* —Tony Shalhoub, from the movie *How Do You Know*

**Most people you meet** don't know what they want in life and business. If they do know, they don't ask for what they want! Why is that? Well, there are a number of things that hold them back from living the life they want. I've observed seven sad reasons why most people stay stuck in lives of quiet desperation—in no particular order:

1) They have never actually thought about what they really wanted.
2) No one told them they could.

3) They don't believe they are worth it.

4) It's uncomfortable, even scary to them.

5) They are afraid to ask. What if I fail?

6) They are worried about what other people will think.

7) No one they know does it.

Barbara Sher, in her book *Wishcraft*, says: *"You must go after your wish. As soon as you start to pursue a dream, your life wakes up and everything has meaning—and our dreams are who we are. Every single one of us can do things that no one else can do—can love things that no one else can love. We are like violins. We can be used for doorstops, or we can make music. You know what to do."*

What do YOU wish and want?

I have been setting goals on three-by-five cards since I was fourteen years old. Mind you, I didn't achieve every one. If I'm honest, I achieved forty percent of them at best. But if I were a professional baseball player, that would a .400 batting average.

As a teenager, I read my first sports biography. My hero was Ted Williams. When he was seventeen years old he set a lifetime goal. *"After I retire from base-ball, as I walk down the street, I want to hear people say: 'There goes the greatest hitter in the history of base-ball!'"* That stuck with me.

Not since 1941 has anyone in baseball completed a season with a batting average of .400 or higher. Eighty years! Boston Red Sox slugger and Hall of Famer Ted Williams was the last to accomplish this feat. And he crossed the threshold in an unforgettable performance. The 1941 season ended for the Red Sox on Sept. 28. The Red Sox were in Philadelphia playing a doubleheader against the Athletics. Boston defeated Philadelphia in both games, ending the season in second place in the American League. But the Red Sox's two wins were overshadowed by a historic day at the plate for Williams. He played left field for the Red Sox in both games, enter-ing the day with a batting average of .3995—which would be rounded up to .400. His manager wanted him to sit out to secure the record. But Williams insisted on playing to ensure there was no doubt about his mark. Ted Williams hit .406 in 1941, going six-for-eight on the season's last day to raise his average from .3995. The 1941 season was one of the best of Williams's career. In addition to the .406 batting average, he ended the season with thirty-seven home runs and 120 runs batted in. Williams's .553 on-base percentage that season set a single-season record that stood for sixty-one years, surpassed only by Barry Bonds in 2002.

"Ted was the greatest hitter of our era," Hall of Famer Stan Musial said, "He loved talking about hitting and was a great student of hitting and pitchers."

I need to watch the movie *How Do You Know* again. Reese Witherspoon plays a baseball player who struggles with life after softball.

What do you really wish and want in life and business? Ted Williams knew . . .

## Your Ah-has? List Your Lights

*"What do I REALLY want in life?"*

_____

_____

_____

_____

_____

_____

_____

_____

_____

_____

_____

_____

_____

_____

_____

_____

_____

_____

_____

_____

## *Window Forty-Eight*

# WHO *REALLY* MAKES THE BUYING DECISION?

*I've been so lucky to work with such great people: people that are such hard workers and have such a respect and appreciation for one another.* —Blake Lively, actor

**The first year I was married,** my wife Debbie made some changes. Gone were the cinder blocks and planks that held my extensive record collection, along with the coffee table I made in wood shop in high school. They were replaced by an elegant coffee table and a fancy shelf to store my LPs. You see, for a woman, the home is a very personal reflection of her good taste. For a man, it's a place to kick back, relax, and watch the game. Venus vs. Mars.

Years ago, I shared the stage with Sharon Roberts. As we talked in the green room, she asked if I had written any books. I gave her a copy of my first book *Freedom from Fear*. She reciprocated by giving me her book, *Selling To Women & Couples: Secrets of Selling in the New Millennium*. I read it that night in one sitting (It's only eighty-five pages!). In this insightful book, she claims—and I believe it—*"85% of all buying decisions in the home are made by . . . (wait for it!) WOMEN!"* In my house, it's 110%!

Is this a firm, fast rule that applies to every sale? No. It's just eighty-five percent of the time.

You see, SHE is the economic buyer, HE is the feasibility buyer. She can say yes, he can say no. Your close ratio will increase if both SHE and HE are in the room. What is vital to remember is to give her at least, if not more, attention than him. If you disrespect her or simply forget that this simple idea is important, you will lose the sale and never know why.

In my sales seminars, I ask the women in the room, "How many of you have been disrespected by a salesperson when you were with your husband or boy-friend?" EVERY woman raises her hand!

Every person you meet is looking for three simple things: appreciation, respect, and understanding, no exceptions. Remember **A.R.U.** (As in *are you* giving this to everyone you meet?).

## Appreciation

Webster's dictionary defines appreciation as: *Recognition and enjoyment of the good qualities of someone or something.* Dale Carnegie advised his readers, *"Be hearty in your approbation and lavish in your praise of others."* One of my favorite phrases is *Good for you!* when someone tells me they closed a big deal or earned a promotion. I have learned that becoming a GOOD-finder is a fast and simple way to make friends. It's the opposite of criticism. It's a simple celebration of another person's success.

## Respect

Webster's dictionary defines respect as, *A feeling of deep admiration for someone or something elicited by their abilities, qualities or achievements; Due regard for the feelings, wishes, rights and traditions of others."* Walk a mile in someone else's shoes. Go back and remember what it was like to be the new guy at the office, or how hard junior high school was as a gawky teenager with a pimple on your nose. Avoid interrupting others, or worse, *shoulding* on someone. Empathy is a muscle that can grow with use. Be respect-full.

## Understanding

Epictetus once said, *"Nature has given men one tongue and two ears, that we may hear from others twice as much as we speak."* Calvin Coolidge famously said, *"No man ever listened himself out of a job."* Actively listening is how we get to understanding. Like math, there is always another level of awareness. It's amazing what other people will tell you if you are NOT waiting to talk, looking at your phone, staring off into the distance, thinking of what you are going to say next. Just listen without interruption with the goal of understanding their feelings and circumstances.

I have done hundreds of ride-alongs with salespeople. If asked to participate in the sales process, the first thing I do is say to HER, "You have a lovely home . . ." (Appreciation). The second thing is to give HER equal, if not more, eye contact (Respect). The third thing is to listen, *really* listen to what she says (Understanding). When you make these three simple ideas a habit, the sale happens as a matter of course.

I really miss that old coffee table and all those LPs. They have been replaced by elegant furniture and an iPhone with 6,800 songs downloaded.

But you know the old saw, *Happy Wife, Happy Life!* We have been married for forty-one years. That's no accident. Now you know who really makes the decisions.

## Your Ah-has? List Your Lights

*"How can I show A.R.U.?"*

_____

_____

_____

_____

_____

_____

_____

_____

_____

_____

_____

_____

_____

_____

_____

_____

_____

_____

_____

_____

_____

# *Window Forty-Nine*

# UNLEASHING YOUR TALENT

*Repetition. Don't look for the big, quick improvement.*
*Seek the small improvements, one day at a time. That's*
*the only way it happens—and when it happens, it lasts.*
—Daniel Coyle, *The Wisdom of Wooden*

**Is it nature or nurture?** Are we born with natural talents or are they developed over time by hard work and study? *"To gain mastery in any discipline, you simply need to invest 10,000 hours or ten years of hard work."* The key part of that statement is *the hard work.* It's about the struggle. The stopping and the starting, the adjusting and correcting.

My friend Gary is a very successful contractor and developer. He made his fortune in Alaska during the boom times of the 1980s. No one outworks Gary. He claims he only works half-days. "You just need to decide which half you are going to work, a.m. or p.m." He smiles and says, "My work days have twelve hours."

Every once in a while a young person will say to me, "I'd give anything to do what you do! Traveling the world speaking, writing books, that must be amazing!"

I smile and say, "I'm self-employed. When I call in sick, I know I'm lying!" followed closely by, "Anyone can do what I do. You just need to invest ten years, twelve hours a day, and $150,000 in your personal and professional development to earn the K.A.S.H. (Knowledge, Attitude, Skills, Habits). Are you willing to do that? Because that is what I did."

They usually say, "I can't do that, that's crazy!" Then they hang up the phone or walk away. What they are really saying is, "I want to do what you do without putting in the time, effort, and resources to earn my place at the table."

If you are still reading, let's roll up our sleeves and get to work. Here is the formula for mastery. It's simple, but not easy.

1) **Ignition**
2) **Coaching**
3) **Deep Practice**

## Ignition

Ignition is exactly what it sounds like, as in, "Ignition, blast off!" It's the lighting of a match. It's the fire in the belly. It's the inspirational dissatisfaction; being sick and tired of being sick and tired. It's hitting bottom. It's saying, "Enough of this! I'm going to change, come hell or high water!" I was cut from my junior high basketball team in eighth grade. I was so mad. I truly believed I should have made the roster. It's really the story of three boys, Mark, Dale and Dan. Mark and Dale both got cut; Dan made the team. Dan was an early bloomer, he had muscles. He was done growing. Dale was simply not a good basketball player, though he thought he was. After he was cut, he gave up. He stuck with football and track. Mark, on the other hand, was a late bloomer and young for his grade (If you haven't figured out by now, Mark is me!). Mark got mad. He made a decision. "No matter what, I am going to make the team next year. I'll pay any price." He approached the best player in his grade, Ken, and asked, "How did you get so good at basketball?"

Ken replied, "I shoot two hours every day and go to Bob Houbregs Basketball Camp every summer!" Ignition, blast off! Mark earned the money to go to camp, mowing lawns, washing windows, etcetera. At camp he learned *what* to practice in his two-hour commitment and received valuable playing time and great ideas from coaches and mentors. In addition, over the next nine months, he read every book he could find on basketball, devoured sports pages and magazines, hit every open gym at night and, oh yes, engaged in deep practice over two hours a day, every day. You guessed it: He made the team the next year. Dale did not. Neither did Dan. Motivation is subjective. It's personal. It's proving someone wrong. It's having a reason, a big hairy emotional reason, followed by hard work. Rain or shine, it's putting in the time to get better, every day.

## Coaching

Coaches have been where you want to go and done what you want to do. They are teachers who have a passion for helping other people on their journey, mostly because they know what it's like to be cut, to be told you are not good enough. It's a kind of *Magnificent Obsession* (read the book by Lloyd C. Douglas) fueled by empathy and understanding. Coaches save you time and money. They assist in offering up short cuts, insights, ideas, strategies, and motivation. They say things like, "If you take one step, I'll take two!" They not only offer up great ideas, they also foster the belief that you CAN do it! *If only.*

If only you follow a simple set of guidelines. If only you put in the time. If only you give up other things in pursuit of your dreams. If only you work harder than anyone else you know. If only you persist. If only you push past the pain. If only you work hard, *deep practice.* When you get frustrated, they lift you up. When you put in the time and effort, they praise your efforts and encourage you to keep going. They care about you. They want you to succeed. Sometimes they come from the least likely places. It might be a math teacher who shows you how simple "cross-multiply and divide" really is. Or an uncle who played college ball and shows you what he used to do. Or an older neighbor boy who sees the passion in your eyes and takes you under his wing. When you feel like quitting, they talk you out of it. They are angels really, sent to you from God to light the way. Saints helping the sinners. Dads inspiring their sons. Mothers teaching their daughters. Dutch uncles telling you the hard truths to instruct and inspire you to grand and noble heights.

## Deep Practice

Ask any Olympic athlete how much time they put in, they will tell you, "Oh, five hours a day, seven days a week, for eight or nine years. I gave up going to parties, hanging out with friends, going to the mall." You see, they paid the price in advance and sacrificed a great deal for their mastery.

Five years ago, I was walking through the brand-new state-of-the-art student center at the University of Louisville preparing to deliver a team building seminar for the women's crew team. The head of facilities asked me if I needed anything. I entered her office and was introduced to two students, a young man and a young woman.

I smiled, shook hands, and then did a double-take. "Kelsi Worrell? How was Rio?" You see, this young lady had just returned from the Olympics where her 4 x 100 Medley Relay team had won the gold medal. Kelsi Worrell, a four-time NCAA champion and Honda Cup Award winner is the first Louisville Cardinal to win a swimming medal of any color. In short, she is a Golden Cardinal. I congratulated her on her success and asked her if she wouldn't mind answering some questions from the women's crew team for ten to fifteen minutes. She graciously agreed to. I lobbed a couple of easy questions to get her started and from there the questions flowed like Niagara Falls. It was a wonderful twenty minutes. She is so humble and kind. Here are the highlights:

## TEAMWORK

She was quick to point out how great her teammates were and that any success was the team's success. It's the *window-and-mirror* principle. When it comes time to assume the credit, you look out the window and give it away to your team. When it's time to assume blame, you look in the mirror.

## JOURNALING

She was proud to report she kept a journal all thirty-six days in Rio. It helped her capture the WINS and SETBACKS (she placed ninth in a solo race) providing her with objectivity, perspective, and recall.

## INTENTION

She set very specific short and long-term goals for herself. She visualized achieving those goals every day for years. She celebrated her WINS to give her confidence and analyzed her TEMPORARY SETBACKS to gather up the lessons they provided (deep practice!). She was very focused. She possessed a burning desire to succeed.

## HARD WORK

Sacrifice. Reps. Discipline. It meant giving up things that most women her age enjoy and take for granted. Delayed gratification. It was time in the pool every day, competing against the best in the country. "YOU just have to put in the time every day, one day at a time. You have to earn it!" she said with a smile. There it is again, deep practice!

## MEASURE

Where performance is measured, performance improves. She knew exactly how many kicks per pool length were required. By measuring her progress she was able to improve the little things that cut her time down.

## GRATITUDE

She shared that she knew it was a privilege to be in the Olympics and also said she knew she wasn't going to be able to swim forever. "All this is temporary, so it's important to enjoy the journey. Soak it all in." She was genuinely thankful for the opportunity to compete at the highest level against the greatest athletes in the world.

## FAITH

She is very spiritual and gave the credit to her mother for infusing the faith in God required to push through setbacks, frustrations, and injuries (coaching!). She is so sincere and genuine. Smiling constantly, yet with a large measure of humility and grace.

It's clear she has an incredible future ahead of her. I told her as much. "Your future is so bright it burns my eyes." I thanked her for making the time and the extraordinary women's crew team were pleasantly surprised by her impromptu Q&A. It added so much to our time together. It was also a wonderful reinforcement of the principles I had been sharing, almost like an echo. The difference was, the words and principles were coming from a Golden Cardinal.

I played some cribbage with Gary last night. He beat me three games to one. He is seventy-three years young. Do you aspire to unleash your talent? Take a page from Gary's book. He still only works half-days. He is going to outlive us all . . .

## Your Ah-has? List Your Lights

*"Am I willing to work half days? A.M. or P.M.?"*

_____

_____

_____

_____

_____

_____

_____

_____

_____

_____

_____

_____

_____

_____

_____

_____

_____

_____

_____

_____

# Window Fifty

# MEMBERS ONLY?

*Clothes make the man. Naked people have little or no influence on society.* —Mark Twain

**They say, "Clothes make the man,"** (whoever *they* are). Fashion is a funny thing. Every five years or so, something new comes into style and something old goes out of style. Popular culture plays a big part in those trends. Are you old enough to remember when Don Johnson starred in *Miami Vice?* Seemingly overnight, pink t-shirts with a white sport coat and fancy shoes without socks became all the rage. One night I had dinner with my parents, it must have been 1987. I was wearing a pink t-shirt with a sport coat and slacks, no socks. My father looked down at my feet and said, "Did you forget to wear some socks?"

He couldn't believe that was a conscious decision on my part.

In 1975, a brand-new jacket was created and introduced to the American markets in1980 by Europe Craft Imports in New York City (which, along with Paris, is where most trends begin). *Members Only* was known in the 1980s for their shift from celebrity endorsements as a form of advertisement, to public service announcements regarding issues like anti-drugs and pro-voting. Members of La Cosa Nostra were known for wearing this type of jacket in the 1980s and 1990s. Members Only racer jackets were distinguished by their narrow épaulettes and collar straps and their knitted trim; they were manufactured in a wide variety of colors. Their advertising tagline was, "When you put it on, something happens!"

When we see those jackets now, they're usually worn by a guy in his seventies who still believes he looks great. He is in a kind of time warp. You know the guy, he also sports a really bad toupee that flips up in the back and doesn't match his actual hair color. We all know he is bald and hopelessly out of style. Something's happening alright!

In the mid-2000s, I had put on a lot of weight, fifty pounds to be exact. I noticed that men my age were wearing a lot of long, untucked, multi-colored striped shirts, along with a black t-shirt, with designer jeans and brown dress shoes with tassels. I bought a bunch of those shirts. The message? Okay, I'm fat but hip. Stripes, you see, are slimming! If I am honest, most of my sartorial choices come from men's fashion magazines and guys I see in airports. Once I lost the weight and got fit, I lost the long shirts and went with tight fitting polo shirts and black t-shirts, you know, to show off the guns! I still don't wear socks most of the year. Thanks, Crockett!

We used to have "casual Fridays" when we could wear jeans to work along with a Hawaiian shirt. As long as the shoes and belt matched, we were good. Today, my oldest son, who works at Amazon, wears a t-shirt with a logo (*Upper Left USA* is real popular in the Northwest) and stocking cap. The Amazonians consider that dressing up. You almost never see a tie or a sport coat anymore. I recently watched a video of Jeff Bezos giving a keynote speech at Century Link Field with 70,000 employees. He wore jeans and a blue button-down dress shirt.

What determines the choices we make when it comes to clothes?

1) Magazines
2) Celebrity choices (Think Pharrell Williams wearing that forest ranger hat!)
3) Television shows
4) Movies
5) Musicians
6) Comfort zones of your reference group (high school, college, corporations)
7) Trends (When did every girl or woman from age twelve to thirty-two start wearing ripped jeans and black Spanx?)
8) Family and friends
9) Corporate norms

We join the group out of fear. Fear of criticism. Of not fitting in and being accepted into our reference groups. We go along to get along. We want to be accepted.

My senior year in high school, Katie McDevitt, our homecoming queen, also earned *best dressed* in our high school graduating class. I never saw her wear the same outfit twice! When she invited me to be her date for prom, I asked her, "Where do you get all your clothes?" (She came from a family of eight and they were not rich). She smiled and replied, "I get most of my clothes at Goodwill and Salvation Army!" I was shocked.

Why do you wear what you wear? You can still buy a Members Only jacket on Amazon. But do you really want to? Just because you can doesn't mean you should!

What did I do with that *Miami Vice* VHS tape? I want to see Crocket and Tubbs crushing it! Members Only . . .

## Your Ah-has? List Your Lights

*"Why do I wear what I wear?"*

_____

_____

_____

_____

_____

_____

_____

_____

_____

_____

_____

_____

_____

_____

_____

_____

_____

_____

_____

*Window Fifty-One*

# SHOULD CHILDREN BE SEEN AND NOT HEARD?

*Children have never been very good at listening to their elders, but they have never failed to imitate them.*
—James Baldwin

**When I was growing up,** I heard my parents say certain things over and over again. If they said it once, they said it a hundred times! I'm not certain where these phrases came from, perhaps they heard their parents say them, or other parents, or in magazines or books they read. Who knows? But hear them I did, many times. Some were filled with wisdom and hard-earned experience; others were simply ridiculous, even insulting. At the top of the list?

*Children should be seen and not heard!* W.T.H.? (What the heck?). If you want to build your child's self-esteem and worth, that is not on the list of suggested quotes. In other words, what I heard was: "Shut up and listen!" or, "You aren't old enough to have anything worthwhile to say!" or, "You haven't earned your place at the table!"

Here are a few more nuggets of negativity from the sixties:

**"It might not be new, but at least it's clean!"** (My father used to say that to me when he was washing his car). The problem with that one? "It's okay to be poor." Or, "I don't make enough money to buy a new car, like some of your wealthy friends' parents do."

**"Charity begins at home!"** (Dad would say that when someone asked him for a charitable donation for the Girl Scouts or a Little League team). He was really saying, "I don't believe in helping those less fortunate than me."

When I became a father, I decided to search for and find ideas and information that would build my children's worth and esteem. In my search I found a story by

Jack Canfield that I shared with my wife. Jack's next-door neighbor, David, was teaching his seven-year-old son, Kelly, to use a gas-powered lawn mower. When Jan, David's wife, called from across the yard, Kelly turned his head and mowed a two-foot-wide swath through the flowerbed . . .

*David had put a lot of time and effort into making those flower beds the envy of the neighborhood. The moment his voice climbed higher in a semi-rage toward poor Kelly, Jan walked quickly over to him, put her hand on his shoulder and said, "David, please remember . . . we're raising children, not flowers!"*

Some of my other favorite positive quotes:

*There are only two lasting bequests we can hope to give our children. One of these is roots, the other, wings.*

*It is easier to build strong children than to repair broken men.*

*Don't worry that children never listen to you; worry that they are always watching you.*

Don't get me wrong. It's not that my parents did a lousy job raising us. We always had three squares a day, a roof over our heads, and clothes on our backs. And some of the positive things they said and did were helpful, like:

*A place for everything and everything in its place.*

*Your mother and I might not always agree, but we made a decision to stay together, no matter what (And they did).*

*You practice how you play!* (Dad's advice on basketball practice).

To my father's credit, he always showed up on time for work, did his job, kept his promise to give up drinking, and would always come to my games. He was a very different guy after he gave up John Barleycorn. What I would give for just one more day with both he and "me mum." They weren't perfect, no parents are. They did the best job they could, based on their awareness. As grandparents to my boys, they were loving, kind, generous, and warm.

Today, I believe my granddaughters should be *seen* and *heard* and *hugged* and *praised* for their efforts, struggles, and resilience. In fact, their future is so bright, it burns my eyes. That's what I told their parents. Guess what? I wear shades when I visit.

Our granddaughters WANT to see us. The other day, I Facetimed Penny Pie. She said, "Boppa, I want you to come to our house!"

My wife said, "We will on Tuesday!"

She replied, "No, I want you to come <u>on today!</u>" Priceless. How sad would that have been if I didn't want to *hear* or *see* her?

What do you say to your employees? What we SAY and DO matters.

## Your Ah-has? List Your Lights

*"What do I say to my children and grandchildren?"*

_____

_____

_____

_____

_____

_____

_____

_____

_____

_____

_____

_____

_____

_____

_____

_____

_____

## *Window Fifty-Two*

# DO AFFIRMATIONS WORK?

**What is an affirmation?** According to Webster, it's *The action or process of affirming something or being affirmed.* It's a declaration, a proclamation, a decision exclaimed aloud, a target to hit.

It really is true, *We become what we think about!*

What few people understand or appreciate is that the mind is like a garden. It will grow whatever you plant. It doesn't care. It's neutral. So what are you planting?

Are you aware of what you say, either silently or aloud to yourself or others? Words trigger pictures and bring about emotion. Each of us has over sixty thousand thoughts a day and seventy-five percent of them are both negative and habitual. With enough repetition, those emotionalized words transform us, to a heaven or a hell on earth. Your self-talk matters. G.I.G.O. = Garbage In, Garbage Out. Managing our self-talk will help or hurt, depending upon the habitual use of positive or negative words and phrases. If we say something often enough with the corresponding emotional impact, it becomes a new belief.

There is a big difference between *I'm terrified of speaking in public* and *I love speaking to large groups, the bigger the better!* Words trigger pictures and bring about emotion and lead to results.

It's been said *The number-one fear people have is public speaking.* That means most people would rather be in the casket that deliver the eulogy! I'd rather deliver the eulogy.

The first time I tried using affirmations consistently, and with a very specific purpose, I was fourteen years old. "Just do it as a test," my mentor said, "for thirty days. If anything positive happens, do it for another thirty days." So I did.

I was told to focus on one simple basketball goal: *I dominate the backboards and rip the ball off the glass. Twelve rebounds per game!* I put that sentence on three-by-five cards and placed them everywhere. I said them aloud five-to-six times a day with positive emotion. In three weeks I went from scrub to star on the court. It was a revelation. I had nine rebounds in one quarter, a school record! It changed my mind and my life. I then applied it to school and grades. I went from a 1.8 GPA to a 3.8 GPA in one semester. It was a **C.B.A.** moment: **C**onceive, **B**elieve, **A**chieve.

You see, your self-image is a kind of thermostat setting. It controls your comfort zones. If you set a thermostat to seventy degrees Fahrenheit, it will maintain a comfort zone of four degrees, between sixty-eight and seventy-two. It's called a *dead-band*. If you change the setting, you changed the dead-band/comfort zone. Your self-image isn't fixed; just like the thermostat, it can be changed. Up or down, cooler or hotter. You have a set point regarding how much money you make, the kind of driver you are, the kind of parent or manager you are.

**Conscious - Subconscious - Creative Subconscious**

## Conscious

Your conscious process allows you to accomplish simple things, like walking or talking or making decisions. As explained by neuropsychologist Paul D. Nussbaum in 2010, "the cortex is also responsible for the most complex thinking abilities, including memory, language, planning, concept formation, problem solving, spatial representation, auditory and visual processing, mood, and personality." Cortex processing is **conscious**; it is intentional.

## Subconscious

The subconscious stores information like a memory stick or a white board. Its job is capture input and assist in simple daily routines. Positioned beneath the cortex, the more primitive subcortex "primarily processes rote skills and procedures" with most of the processing being subconscious. Examples of **subconscious** activities are word processing, tying your shoes, typing on a keyboard, and driving—things we do habitually. The cortex and subcortex connect in many ways and work very effectively together.

## Creative Subconscious

The creative subconscious makes certain we "act like us." It keeps us in our comfort zones. Once the setting has been changed, it seeks information and feedback that has been stored in the subconscious to alter our performance. It's the HOW part of our brain. Like cruise control in your car, it adjusts and corrects according to the setting, faster, slower.

My junior year of high school basketball, I shot sixty-five percent from the free-throw line. Leveraging what I had learned about goals, I wrote out a series of new affirmations, one of them concerned free throws. ("Who gets to shoot the other team's technical fouls? The best free-throw shooter!"). So I wrote *"I enjoy an eighty-five percent free-throw average. I shoot one hundred free throws a day!"*

Any new goal needs to be backed up by continuous action. Every day that summer, rain or shine, I shot one hundred free throws. I created muscle memory and *myelin* (a kind of pathway between my sub-conscious and creative subconscious to make certain my elbow was in and I followed through on every shot). One game, mid-season in my senior year, I hit 15-15 free throws. I changed my setting and corresponding comfort zone. The results followed. What is amazing to me, after all these years, is I can still make better than eight out of ten free throws. It's how I see myself.

Early on in my professional speaking career, a fellow speaker, Andrew Bennett, shared some speaking goals with me, simple affirmations. There were about seven of them. I typed them up, printed them out, and put them everywhere, just as I had done twenty-two years before with basketball. As my awareness and experience evolved, I would add one or two new ones. To date, there are twenty-seven affirmations and I say them every day. Most of them I've said thousands of times. Why? They work! They have improved my self-image, confidence, skills, attitude, performance and, oh yes, my income.

## Mark Matteson – International Keynote Speaker
### *Affirmations*

☐ *I am an inspirational and <u>dynamic</u> speaker; I build rapport in minutes!*

☐ *I <u>astonish</u> my audiences with my passion, preparation, humor, knowledge, extra-mile* *delivery, and other-centered philosophy (I am a go-giver!).*

☐ *I <u>love</u> what I do and it shows; I have a passion for working with others!*

☐ *I <u>tell great stories</u> and others love hearing them!*

☐ *I have <u>charisma</u> and a kind of casual confidence.*

☐ *I am at <u>ease</u> in front of thousands of people!*

☐ *My <u>enthusiasm</u> pulls people into the learning. I was born for this work! I am passionate about my life's work.*

☐ *I deliver with the utmost sincerity, conviction, and <u>humility</u>. I am authentic, real. My audiences really connect and relate to me!*

☐ *I am making a <u>huge</u> difference in <u>my clients' profitability</u> and overall health. My clients prosper and refer me to other great clients!*

☐ *I naturally use <u>hand gestures to match my message</u>.*

☐ *Standing ovations and Invitations are the norm. I deliver world-class presentations!*

- ☐ *I habitually use my <u>natural voice</u> at all times. It's at once both soothing and inspiring. I smoothly blend flawless imitations of famous people into my presentations.*

- ☐ *I easily and deftly use <u>improv</u> and the 'genius of AND' to:*
  *>Acknowledge and heighten*
  *>Stay other centered*
  *>Paraphrase forward emotions and thoughts*
  *>Call back to specific client details*

- ☐ *I am a world-class public active listener. I <u>summarize</u> my audience's core concerns, feelings, and issues.*

- ☐ *My audiences feel <u>understood</u>, respected, and appreciated.*

- ☐ *I focus on <u>innovation</u> and raising the bar.*

- ☐ *I deliver <u>nuggets</u>, poignant messages that can be easily remembered.*

- ☐ *I am genuine and real in a humble way. <u>Authenticity!</u> I use self-effacing humor that puts people at ease.*

- ☐ *I consistently use a 'powerful pause' to <u>let my audience breathe.</u> My timing is world-class.*

☐ *I have accepted my humanness and faults so that <u>others feel safe around me!</u>*

☐ *I am prepared because I use lists, outlines, forms, and processes. I am a <u>master</u> presenter!*

☐ *I am a voracious reader and <u>student of presentation</u>. I watch videos, read books, listen to audios/CDs and solicit feedback from clients to improve. <u>I love to learn</u>. I am a serious student of platform skills and content. I borrow boldly from the best.*

☐ *I prowl the stage like a panther, move in and out of the audience, interacting with people. My <u>impersonations</u> of Charlie Jones, my English mother, Marlon Brando, Rod Serling, JFK, and Arnold Schwarzenegger are seamless and effective.*

☐ *I ask for repeat business and with my back-of-the-room sales at the end of my talks; money and new opportunities flow to me like water!*

☐ *It's fun and easy for me to deliver seventy-five presentations a year around the globe. I love to travel!*

I keep adding to the list as new ideas and insights pop up.

Let me be clear: Affirmations only work if you REALLY, REALLY WANT THE THING YOU ARE AFFIRMING! In for a dime, in for a dollar. Making a decision to manifest the thing you've written down is like "turning the glass over!" Like the winner in a drinking contest, the slam of the glass is an affirmation; it says, I won! (Full disclosure: I quit drinking over forty-one years ago, but I've slammed my fair share of glasses!).

The secret to life is: *"Figure out what you want and learn how to ask for it!"*

What is it you want?

1) Choose an area in your life you would like to improve.
2) Write it down on paper. I have used three-by-five cards because they are portable and easy to carry around in my wallet.
3) *"How much? By when?"* Make it measurable and time-sensitive.

4) Remember to format them using the Four Ps of Affirmations: Personal, Positive, Powerful, Present-tense!

5) Notice the structure of my speaking affirmations: They begin with "I AM . . ." or "I HAVE . . ." ("I WILL . . ." doesn't work).

6) It's a positive lie. It's a new Be-LIE-f! It's where you are going, not where you are.

7) Remember **R.E.T.** (**R**epetition, **E**motion, **T**ime). Reps will change your self-Image with patience and persistence. It's how we learn anything (Can you say the Pledge of Allegiance? Uh-huh . . .).

8) Keep your goals to yourself at first, with the exception of people who can help you achieve them (mentors, coaches, positive friends).

9) Make a list of *why* you want that goal. What are your *reasons?* Our *whys* pull us to the future. They emotionalize the goal.

10) Commit to saying them aloud five to ten times a day for thirty days as a test. If anything positive happens, do it for another thirty days (By the way, the more often you say them each day, and the stronger the emotion, the faster they will manifest in your life).

Would I have done seventy-five speaking engage-ments a year around the world for the last twenty-five years if I hadn't affirmed the declarations I listed above? I doubt it.

*My favorite affirmation when I feel stuck or out of sorts is: "Whatever I need is already here, and it is all for my highest good!" Jot this down and post it conspicuously throughout your home, on the dashboard of your car, at your office, on your microwave oven, and even in front of your toilets!* —Wayne Dyer, author, speaker, philosopher

*Make New Year's goals. Dig within and discover what you would like to have happen in your life this year. This helps you do your part. It is an affirmation that you're interested in fully living life in the year to come.* —Melodie Beatty, author, speaker

*You will be a failure until you impress the subconscious with the conviction you are a success. This is done by making an affirmation which 'clicks.'* —Florence Scovel Shinn, author

*I have a dream (affirmation) that my four little children will one day live in a nation where they will not be judged by the color of their skin, but by the content of their character.* —Martin Luther King, Jr.

If you are an aspiring speaker, consider borrowing five to ten of my affirmations. After all, I borrowed them from my buddy Andrew Bennett, a two-time TED Talk Phenom. It all began for with those "Magnificent Seven" he sent me.

Once you begin to enjoy the success that working smart and affirming what you want in life brings, share your experience, strength, and hope with others. It's called *dual-plane learning.* You get to hear it again as you share what you know with others. In and of itself, it's also an affirmation, one of abundance.

As professional speakers, we are privileged to *"Turn our mess into a message!"* as Judy Carter says. What a great gig! In every book I sign after a keynote speech I also write an affirmation. It says simply *"The best is yet to come!"* I pluck thistles and plant roses where I think they might grow . . .

## Suggested Reading List (Both Old & New Books)

- ❑ *Freedom from Fear,* by Mark Matteson
- ❑ *The Talent Code,* by Daniel Coyle
- ❑ *Atomic Habits,* by James Clear
- ❑ *Think and Grow Rich,* by Napoleon Hill
- ❑ *How to Stop Worrying and Start Living,* by Dale Carnegie
- ❑ *The 7 Habits of Highly Effective People,* by Stephen Covey
- ❑ *Goals,* by Brian Tracy
- ❑ *Write it Down, Make it Happen,* by Henriette Klauser
- ❑ *The Greatest Salesman in the World.* by Og Mandino
- ❑ *The Magic of Thinking Big,* by David J. Schwartz
- ❑ *The Magic of Believing,* by Claude M. Bristol
- ❑ *It's about TIME,* by Mark Matteson
- ❑ *Creative Visualization,* by Shakti Gawain
- ❑ *Chop Wood Carry Water,* by Joshua Medcalf
- ❑ *What Got You Here Won't Get You There,* by Marshall Goldsmith
- ❑ *Psycho-cybernetics,* by Maxwell Maltz

## Your Ah-has? List Your Lights

*"What affirmations will take me where I want to go?"*

_____

_____

_____

_____

_____

_____

_____

_____

_____

_____

_____

_____

_____

_____

_____

_____

_____

_____

_____

_____

# AFTERWORD

*Set your goals high, and don't stop till you get there.*
—Bo Jackson

**Goals add years to our lives and life to our years.** First we work on goals, then they work on us. I will never stop setting goals. I wrote poems for my granddaughter after she was born. I have written many more since then. In a very real sense, this book is for all my grandchildren. My sincere hope is that the ideas in this book serve to assist them in navigating the rapids of change and offer solutions to life's challenges.

Here are some old lights for your new windows, little ones. These lessons came to me, some from painful personal experience, and others vicariously through the pain of others.

Boppa loves you!

*I love you all more today than yesterday, but not as much as tomorrow. Life isn't always fair, but it's always good. Life is too short for hating. Take your work seriously, but not yourself. When you are wrong, promptly admit it—*

*when you are right, remain silent. Make peace with your past, savor the present, dream big dreams for the future. It's okay to let your children see you cry. Compare and compete with your own best self. Stop comparing yourself to others. Memory and Imagination are powerful twin pillars of goal achievement! Every year, get a check-up from the neck up! People don't care how much you know, until they know how much you care! It really is true, you can have everything you want in life, everything you want, if you just help enough other people get what they want, FIRST! If a relationship has to be a secret, you shouldn't be in it. Life is too short for long pity parties; get busy living or get busy dying. Over-prepare, then trust yourself. No one is in charge of your happiness except you. Forgive everyone, but remember the lesson. With every disaster faced, ask yourself, "Will this matter in five years?" What other people think of me is none of my business. Everyone is always glad to see me, some when I arrive and some when I leave. Time heals almost everything—it takes time. Knocked down seven times, stand up eight! Growing old beats the alternative—dying young! Get outside and go for a walk, miracles await. The best is yet to come.*

*Get up, suit up, show up, and climb up. Remember to breathe. Only one life that soon is past, only what's done with love will last.*

I'd like to end this book where it began—with a quote from George Bernard Shaw. It summarizes how I feel about life.

*This is the true joy in life, the being used for a purpose recognized by yourself as a mighty one; the being a force of nature instead of a feverish, selfish little clod of ailments and grievances complaining that the world will not devote itself to making you happy.*

*I am of the opinion that my life belongs to the whole community, and as long as I live it is my privilege to do for it whatever I can.*

*I want to be thoroughly used up when I die, for the harder I work the more I live. I rejoice in life for its own sake. Life is no "brief candle" for me. It is a sort of splendid torch which I have got hold of for the moment, and I want to make it burn as brightly as possible before handing it on to future generations.*

## Your Ah-has? List Your Lights

*"The best is truly yet to come . . ."*

_____

_____

_____

_____

_____

_____

_____

_____

_____

_____

_____

_____

_____

_____

_____

_____

_____

_____

_____

_____

# ABOUT MARK MATTESON

**Mark Matteson** is an international speaker and the author of the bestselling book *Freedom from Fear* which has sold over 150,000 copies worldwide. He has written six books and ten eBooks. He is one of those rare professionals who can say he is speaker, consultant, podcaster, publisher, and author and *mean* it. He has attracted clients like Microsoft, Honda, Fujitsu, Daikin, Mitsubishi, T-Mobile, John Deere, Conoco-Phillips, Aflac, Honeywell, and other Fortune-100 companies on three continents. He has been called "an edu-tainer," "an oracle of optimism," "a superlative street scholar," and "an intense idea-reporter." Mark travels 250 days a year around the globe, delivering seventy-five key-notes, seminars, and workshops a year. He is a gifted sto-ryteller, using self-effacing humor, high levels of interac-tion, and powerful and proven business principles to in-spire audiences to the highest levels of productivity and profit. Mark leaves audiences wanting more.

Mark began his career in HVAC in 1976. He has been married to Debbie for forty-one years and has three grown sons and three grandchildren.

**He takes great pride in the fact that he once flunked high scool English!**

**Mark Matteson**
**Bestselling Author, International Speaker**

**To order one of my books, go to**
**www.SparkingSuccess.net/store**

**Phone: 206.697.0454**

**To subscribe to Mark's monthly ezine, go to**
**Mark@SparkingSuccess.net**

**To watch a few short videos,**
**visit https://tinyurl.com/8e7udabj**

## To Listen to my Podcasts, visit:

**Google Play:** https://tinyurl.com/5n5b5ydn

**Apple:** https://tinyurl.com/4zvvyy

*"Make it a great day . . . unless you have other plans!"*

Made in the USA
Monee, IL
10 November 2021

81772085R00193